TRAUMA CENTER

Also by Randall Sword

EMERGENCY ROOM

TRAUMA CENTER

Three Days in the Life of an Emergency Room Doctor

RANDALL S. SWORD, M.D.
and JANET KELLER

CHARLES SCRIBNER'S SONS · NEW YORK

Although the hospital, patients, families, physicians, and emergency room personnel described in this book are composites and therefore fictitious, the events are based on Dr. Sword's experiences as the director of a metropolitan hospital emergency room.

Library of Congress Cataloging in Publication Data

Sword, Randall.
Trauma center.

1. Hospitals—Emergency service. 2. Hospitals—
United States—Emergency service. 3. Sword, Randall.
4. Emergency physicians—United States—Biography.
I. Keller, Janet. II. Title.
RA975.5.E5S89   1984   362.1'8   84–10523
ISBN 0–684–18190–8

1 3 5 7 9 11 13 15 17 19   F/C   20 18 16 14 12 10 8 6 4 2

Printed in the United States of America.

For all the sick and injured and lonely people living on the edge . . . for whom the emergency room is so often the only open door.

CONTENTS

ACKNOWLEDGMENTS

To Cindy Garcia, our consulting editor, whose blue pencil seemed to have a life of its own . . . and to Stuart Fordham for lending a sensitive, perceptive ear.

THE WHITE CORRIDOR

As I enter the corridor from x-ray and walk toward the nurses' station, I hear hot cracking static emanating from the biocom, the special telephone on which we receive information about trauma victims being transported here to the emergency room at Los Angeles Memorial. Moving closer, I listen to the female dispatcher's voice: "Gunshot victim, chest wound, en route to L.A. Memorial. Pulse palpable, blood pressure sixty over zero; victim gasping for breath; paramedics assisting respiration. ETA: three minutes."

At once I feel my muscles tighten, along with a sharpening of awareness. My movements and posture change, too. This happens every time I know the RAs (rescue ambulances) are on their way with a trauma victim.

I have waited here so often in this place I have come

to think of as "the white corridor," listening for the ambulances and police cars.

I don't know why my mind has named it "the white corridor." It certainly isn't white. The walls are a dull, faded green, and the floor is an asphalt-tile shade of nothing. Maybe it's because most of the people who move up and down this corridor wear white: the doctors in white starched coats over green scrub suits, and the technicians and nurses in their white uniforms. If a gurney is parked in the corridor, as it frequently is, it's covered with a white sheet.

Or maybe it's because of the quality of light. Five fluorescent tubes in the ceiling illuminate the corridor. One of them is usually flickering. Flickering fluorescent light, a lighting engineer once told me, can give a stroboscopic effect, making things look surreal.

In the white corridor, shadows sometimes seem to disappear; instruments glitter too brightly; faces turn into masks.

There are no windows, so the light is the same at eight o'clock in the morning as it is at midnight, although nights in the white corridor have a different feel, a different texture than the days. Perhaps because at night—for some people in this city—we are the only open door.

Out of the corner of my eye I see one of the nurses, Illana, move down the corridor and enter the trauma room. It is as instinctive for her to go in there to make certain everything is ready as it is for me to nurture this heightened state of awareness that helps me do my job better: My hands move more swiftly and with greater accuracy; my vision becomes sharper.

Instantly, I can picture the interior of the trauma room. I know it better than I know the living room of my own house. There are two Stryker beds with EKG monitors above each; overhead surgical lamps; a portable x-ray machine; an autotransfuser that will filter a patient's blood and give it back; an arterial blood sampler to read blood gases; a Wright's peak-flow meter that will measure in liters per minute the air a person can push out in one second; a central venous (vein) pressure monitor; supply cupboards filled with the paraphernalia of a trauma room: catheters, tubes, medications, sterile gloves, IV solutions, sutures, instrument packs. Against the wall are trash receptacles—three lined with red bags for infectious waste, and three with blue bags for the rest.

Next to each bed is a crash cart—one with adult-size instruments, the other for children. No matter how many times I use or even just glance at the instruments on the child's crash cart, I am startled by their smallness.

Sy Levine, the other emergency medicine physician on duty this afternoon, comes into the corridor, and his eyes meet mine. He has heard the message on the biocom too. "Want me to call upstairs?" he asks. I nod.

Physicians in all specialties are available at Los Angeles Memorial, or reachable within minutes by phone. When we have a gunshot wound to the chest or abdomen, we alert the cardiovascular surgeon, the OR crew, and the anesthesiologist in the hospital proper. They can get down to ER in minutes, if necessary.

As Sy moves toward the in-hospital phone, he asks if I want him to assist. "Probably," I say, thinking all hands will be needed. I've treated so many bullet wounds in this emergency room during the past four years, I feel as if I must be developing an expertise akin to military physicians in combat zones.

A formula that is permanently engraved in my mind: kinetic energy $= MV^2$ (weight or mass of the bullet times the velocity, squared). Translated into the environ of the

ER, it means bullets injure tissue immediately surrounding the area they penetrate in proportion to the square of their velocity. Twenty-twos, .25s, .32s, even .38s are considered low velocity. Magnum and rifle bullets are high velocity because they carry a higher load and contain more powder. The pathway of a bullet through the body is cone-shaped. A magnum bullet, for example, may enter the body making a hole only one-half inch in diameter, but it can exit through an opening big enough to hold a fist.

I glance down the corridor. The glass panels in the double doors of the ambulance entrance are opaque, covered with wire mesh, and bulletproof. Beyond those doors, a late September sun is shining. It is three-thirty in the afternoon.

Four years ago, when I first came here from a comparatively quiet suburban hospital, I might have asked myself why those doors were bulletproof; why it was necessary to have three security guards on duty twenty-four hours a day and to put a code lock on the doors that open into the waiting room and the hospital proper. I don't ask myself those questions any more. I know why.

If you were to take a city map of Los Angeles and stick pins in it marking the sites of violent occurrences, then draw a circle around the area with the most pins in it, this hospital would be in the middle of the circle. We work in an urban battleground.

Yet we're the only emergency room in the area open to the public. Several hospitals nearby have emergency rooms, but they're not open to rescue ambulances or police cases, or to the public—only to their staff doctors. Several smaller hospitals have closed their ERs or converted them to clinics for daytime use only.

Consequently, we receive more trauma victims than any other private hospital in the county, roughly 700 paramedic and ambulance runs a month. Averaging it out, that's twenty-three a day, one an hour. There may be quiet intervals during the week, but weekends compensate for that; the flow of patients then is nonstop.

You grow here as a physician. You see two, three, four major traumas a day, and you can't help but become better and sharper at your work. However, I'm not sure what happens to the part of you that isn't a doctor.

Sy hangs up the phone as a siren wailing in the distance rises to a crescendo. "Surgeon and OR are alerted," he murmurs.

It will only be seconds now.

I begin to envision the interior of the chest cavity: rib cage, lungs, the pericardial sac that holds the heart. We humans are so intricately put together. Physicians who treat chronic disease often witness the body's awesome recuperative powers brought into play by a consciousness that is given weeks or months to marshal its forces.

But we in the emergency room see the sudden catastrophes that allow the victims no time to gather any strength—the hand mangled by a buzz saw; the near amputations in automobile accidents; the stabbings and gunshot wounds. Here the body must struggle to survive on its own because the consciousness of the person is in the limbo of shock induced by physical trauma.

The siren wail reaches a caterwauling pitch outside our doors and then is abruptly extinguished. The doors slide open. Sunlight silhouettes the figures moving through the ambulance entrance. One paramedic guides the gurney into the corridor, past the doorway of x-ray, as another bag-breathes the victim while yet a third kneels on the gurney performing CPR, the steady rhythmic pumping pressure on the chest to keep the heart beating: down-pause, down-pause, once a second.

The man on the gurney is young, Latin. His shirt and the gurney are soaked with blood.

The paramedic guiding the gurney makes a sharp right turn from the corridor into the trauma room. Four nurses, two respiratory therapists, and three technicians surround the waiting bed, and I am standing at its head. A transfer of responsibility from paramedics to ER staff is about to take place, and it is precisely choreographed.

In a synchronized movement, the ER staff slides the patient from gurney to bed. The paramedic who has been bag-breathing the victim removes the breathing device and steps back, and as he does so I bend over the victim and slide an endotracheal tube down his throat. As soon as I have it in, one of the respiratory therapists moves close to hook the patient up to the breathing machine. The second paramedic continues performing CPR while Illana places on the victim's chest the electrodes that will monitor his heartbeat on the EKG machine. I murmur orders for the injection of adrenaline, calcium, and sodium bicarbonate to correct the metabolic changes occurring from the damaged heart.

Alfred, a second nurse, is inserting an IV catheter in the man's left arm; a third nurse, Eugene, is inserting one in his right. Both IVs will be used for the administration of fluids.

The paramedic who guided the gurney into the trauma room is now wrapping the man's lower body inside a MAST (military antishock trousers) suit, and the one who was doing the bag-breathing moves to the foot of the bed to assist him. The MAST suit functions like a giant blood-pressure cuff. By inflating the suit around the legs and abdomen, three units of the patient's own blood will be autotransfused from his lower body and squeezed up into his torso and head, a maneuver that will give us more time to get him stabilized before an operating team takes over. While the paramedics inflate the MAST suit, one respiratory therapist is suctioning out the victim's throat, the other monitors his breathing; a technician is taking his blood pressure, another is visually monitoring the rhythmic green peak-valley line on the EKG screen above the bed.

I prepare to perform a pericardiocentesis, a surgical puncture of the pericardium, the fibroserous sac which encloses the heart and the roots of the great vessels. This sac is composed of two layers, the parietal and the visceral. When there is trauma to the heart, the normally infinitesimal space between the layers can fill with blood and fluid, compressing the chamber enclosing the heart muscle into an increasingly smaller space, and exerting pressure on the already struggling organ. As I puncture the sac, I hear familiar words exchanged.

"Suction! Jesus, suction him out!"

"This guy's really bleeding out."

"Pulse barely palpable."

"More IVs."

"Let's type and cross, six units STAT!"

"Bring two units of uncrossed blood!"

"Is he breathing?"

I position myself to place a chest tube by making an incision half an inch long just above his sixth rib and directly under his arm. Into this incision I will insert one end of a soft plastic tube about as thick as my little finger between his ribs and into his lung, giving us an opening for drainage. As I cleanse the area under his right arm preparatory to making the incision, I'm aware that two policemen have entered the room, as well as more technicians from the lab upstairs and two med-student volunteers. They form a silent audience.

Abruptly the technician monitoring the EKG announces, "Going flat!"

All eyes turn upward for confirmation. The green line is now horizontal. If we had the machine on audible signal (which we rarely do, because the constant beep, beep, beep is annoying and distracting) it would be emitting a high-pitched whine.

Quickly I assess the signs of life. The man is still gasping for breath. There is no pulse. I'm going to have to crack open the chest. I can't wait for the surgeon from upstairs.

Sy takes my place as team leader at the head of the bed, and I move to the left side of the victim. Illana hands me a no. 10-blade knife from the sterile pack of instruments on the crash cart. Following the contour of the rib cage, I cut through the skin to the startlingly white subcutaneous layer beneath. My knife then slices through the insulating fat, which is almost a topaz yellow. Jewellike globules slide away from the blade, and then the incision I am making opens into flesh, which becomes an entire spectrum of red. The incision is almost fourteen inches long.

Illana hands me the rib spreader, and I insert it between the fifth and sixth ribs. As I crank and turn the rib spreader and the rib cage opens, blood pours out and the lung collapses into velvety softness against my fingers. I push it aside and reach for the tough, sinewy pericardial sac that contains the heart.

All my energy is in my fingertips now.

The exterior of the heart is normally in rhythmic contact with the inner surface of the pericardial sac. But if fluid or blood collects in the pericardium, compressing the heart so that it cannot perform its vital pumping function, the life-threatening condition known as pericardial tamponade develops.

When my fingers touch the sac, it feels like a water-filled balloon. With the pick-up instrument Illana quickly places in my hand, I lift the sac, then slit it its full length along the spinal cord, and the heart is delivered into my hand. Blood drowns my fingers as I reach for, find, and hold the heart in my right hand.

Beginning to squeeze it rhythmically, my fingers slide into a gaping hole in the left ventricle. The bullet went through the heart itself, which means resuscitation is impossible. I cannot understand how the man has clung to life this long.

I step back.

Sy looks at me.

"Bullet tore the heart apart," I murmur.

It takes a few moments for everyone to stop. Like dancers when music is abruptly interrupted, my staff keeps performing for several beats. Almost shyly, then, they begin to look at each other, and then away, and then they stop.

The nurses begin to disengage the catheters; the paramedics remove the MAST suit. I see the surgeon from upstairs standing next to the policemen, silently watching. One of the cops murmurs, "The guy's brother gave him two dollars and sent him to the store for a pound of butter. He got shot for two bucks." The surgeon turns and leaves without saying anything.

Sy disconnects the breathing machine; Illana removes the EKG discs. Gradually, the room empties until only the cleanup nurse remains, who will sheet the body and put the name tag on the "great toe" for the coroner.

Sy and I stand staring down at the collapsed lung in the opened chest. It is beautiful, the softest pink, streaked with the black of a smoker's pollutants; glistening in places, iridescent. It is like a deep-sea creature brought unwillingly to the surface of a bright red sea, exquisite in the act of dying.

Raucous laughter begins to ricochet into the room from the corridor. We turn. Out there, the nurses, the paramedics, and the police are telling each other terrible jokes. I once heard Calvin Bixby, the caustic and erudite ER clerk, comment on this phenomenon. "It's a way to switch back over, from death into life again. We're gamblers covering our losses."

Sy stands beside me quietly for a moment, watching the cleanup nurse and listening to the voices in the corridor. For a second the laughter quiets, then bursts out again louder than before. Sy touches my arm briefly, and leaves.

As I stand watching the cleanup nurse, I wonder, for the hundredth time, why I go on spending my life in these rooms where death defeats us so often. Most of the people I treat are afflicted by poverty, which I consider a disease all its own. They eat substandard diets, live in overcrowded conditions. The incidence of communicable illnesses is high. The number of children born here should be in inverse ratio to unemployment, but it isn't. It's just the opposite. Alcohol and drug abuse is astronomical.

Why do I, or any of us, stay?

I direct a staff of eleven other emergency medicine physicians here at Los Angeles Memorial. There are twenty-eight nurses, five technicians, and twenty-seven clerks who work beside us in this war zone, facing an opponent that can never be beaten, an enemy manifested through despair and hopelessness. The costs to our personal lives are high. Few can come home as we do, drained of energy, reduced to our most elemental needs, and expect any kind of relationship to survive.

"The best part of you," my ex-wife Sandra said, "goes to work. I get whatever is left over."

I don't know that I would agree with "best." "Real"— the most "real" part of me goes to work. Because nowhere, except in the white corridor, do I feel so totally alive, so self-actualized.

Why? I've wondered that for years, and it's a question that's becoming more important to me than any other.

Perhaps if I take one of the days I spend here—and one of the nights, too—examine them, pull them apart, look at their hours and their moments, I might find an answer.

DAY SHIFT

6:00 A.M.—The alarm goes off. I reach a hand out to silence it, realizing, as I come fully awake, that I am alone in the house. A year ago, there were four other people living here: my wife, Sandra; my son, Tod; my daughters, Alexis and Vanessa.

The house is high in the hills above the ocean. It has dark, beamed ceilings, Spanish-tile floors. The spacious rooms are full of windows and sunlight. But as I walk through the house now from the bedroom to the kitchen, it has a curious, almost undressed look, because some of the furniture and pictures are gone. Sandra and I tried to divide what we owned between us. I think now that was a mistake. One of us should have taken it all.

It was "the year," I tell myself, that did it, "the year" in which I tried to crowd too much. I treated the sick and wounded at Los Angeles Memorial, finished writing *Emergency Room*, the book that preceded this one, taught young doctors at the University of Southern California, then studied for and took my examinations to pass the boards in the newly designated specialty of emergency medicine.

Yet now I wonder if it was really "the year," or if it was something more. Was it, in fact, the inescapable rhythm of my life?

Because this is the second time I have failed at marriage.

When my first marriage ended, I managed to convince myself it was because my first wife's life-style and mine were too different. Kathleen and I met and married when we were graduate students. We were both caught up in and determined to help bring about the social reforms the 60s seemed to promise. As that decade's spirit of optimism began to ebb, so did the vitality of our marriage.

I began to believe becoming the best doctor I could be was more important, certainly more attainable, than devoting my energy to righting the world's injustices. Kathleen felt I was betraying causes she still believed in fervently, and our marriage simply and quietly disintegrated.

Now the same thing has happened again—though not simply, and not quietly. And once again my career seems to be the culprit. In that terrible crammed-full year before my marriage to Sandra ended, I would enter my house at whatever odd hour I happened to come home from the hospital—it might be 7:00 A.M., 3:00 P.M., 1:30 A.M.—and I would ask for food if I was hungry (I was always hungry); silence if I was sleepy (I was usually sleepy); sex if I was in the mood (not often in those days).

Something in me must have known Sandra could not go on like that, functioning as a single parent, cook, housekeeper, and occasional wife. But I told myself, "It's just the way things are right now. Soon, everything will change."

6:15 A.M.—I am in the bathroom shaving. I have put the kettle on the burner to heat water for instant coffee. (Sandra used to go to a coffee-bean shop in Palos Verdes, bring home exotic beans, then mix their flavors; I would smell the coffee as I walked into the kitchen. There would be eggs frying too, or French toast browning.)

Breakfasts. How well they sum up the pattern of a life. I remember the rich dark African coffee I drank in the compound in Ethiopia before I began my ten-hour teaching day at the Jesuit-run high school there.

And in later years there was the bowl of cold cereal I'd eat hurriedly before I went to early-morning classes at the University of New Mexico.

And the 4 A.M. coffee and doughnuts I shared with the other med students during exam week as we crammed for our finals.

Suddenly I think of Lorna, who didn't make it, who committed suicide halfway through medical school, and then I try to shut out the memory.

Sy Levine, my friend and co-physician, whom I call "the thinker," wants to know more about Lorna. Sy has a degree in psychology and another in art history. He likes to explore all sorts of boundaries. But I haven't told him much about Lorna, because I don't like to think about what she did or what pushed her to it.

At the beginning of my friendship with Sy, it seemed to me he was preoccupied with too many of the negative things about our profession. He told me, "We have to have an understanding of the dangers, Sword. How many there are, how prevalent they are, how to spot them at a distance. Then if we find ourselves facing one, maybe we'll be able to outmaneuver it."

I go into the kitchen to drink my coffee. There's no butter for my toast; I forgot to buy it. I glance at the calendar on the wall. These days I mark the events on it myself: my shift schedule; the days I have my daughters; appointments with Allen, the therapist I've been seeing since the breakup of my marriage; occasional dates; dinners with Sy. But I know if I lift up the pages, turning to the past, I will see Sandra's handwriting there marking the hours of the days and/or nights I worked, my barber and dental appointments, the parties given by friends she so often had to go to alone.

Today is Thursday. It's also the second-to-last day of the month, which means people will receive their welfare checks on Saturday. Any ER physician working in a metropolitan area has an acute awareness of when people get their welfare checks, because as soon as people start spending their welfare money on the streets, the pace in ER accelerates. And when the checks happen to come out on a Saturday, and the spending starts on a Saturday night, it's bedlam.

I'm on day shift today, Thursday, 7:00 A.M. to 7:00 P.M. Friday I am off. Then I will work night shift on Saturday, 7:00 P.M. to 7:00 A.M.

Most of Saturday I will spend with my daughters. I have drawn large green circles around the days of each month I have them with me. The girls have become oases in my existence, mostly, I suppose, because they are so young that they respond to my love without question; but perhaps also because the only other children I see are sick, hurt, or terrified.

6:25 A.M.—I walk out the door into the early-morning haze September ushers in. A wind from the canyon swirls eucalyptus leaves along the sidewalk. In the driveway my car looks like an intruder. Its paint is grimed; its windows are dull with city smog, and I was so tired when I got home last night, I parked it crookedly.

"Why do I go on living here?" I wonder, watching the mist that is not quite fog. It spreads in from the Pacific, blurring the outlines of bougainvillea and palm trees, lending an aura of fantasy.

I fought hard to keep this house during the divorce settlement, perhaps because I had seen too many doctors in the aftermath of divorce rent bachelor apartments in swinging-singles complexes, and I knew I couldn't do that. Besides, I'd saved the money for the down payment; I'd put up bookshelves, hung pictures, paneled the walls of the den. This is where I want the children to come when they visit me. This is where I live.

Still, the house may be simply an island I cling to in the wake of the dissolution of my marriage, and when the pain of that has gone perhaps I won't need to live here any more. A lot of the time I spend here is "cave" time. I come back simply for shelter, and most of my hours here are spent in the kind of sleep one falls into after a twelve-hour shift at Los Angeles Memorial.

But when I'm awake and moving through the rooms, I'm affected by my house's neglected look. A placid woman named Rowena comes in to clean once a week, but she only touches surfaces. The pillows on the sofa are not plumped; uneaten food turns stale in the refrigerator; magazines are left stacked and unopened.

Sandra would be surprised, I suppose, that I am noticing such things. "You visit us," she accused me. "You drop in once in a while. But you live *there*." She refused to give the hospital a name; she just called it *there*. She may have been right.

My life with Sandra was divided in halves: I might spend the morning watching Alexis and Vanessa laughing as they ran through the spray of sprinklers on our lawn. And that evening, in another world, I'd work on a skull shattered by a bullet, its brain oozing out of the eye sockets.

6:30 A.M.—I back the car out of my driveway and start down the steep, winding road that leads out of my neighborhood. Once away from the hills, I drive six miles over fast surface streets to the freeway, and there I put the car on cruise control. This forty-minute journey to and from the hospital is the one part of the day that is really mine, and I look forward to it. It's a buffer zone between the separate worlds I live in.

Sometimes I'll hear a song from the 60s on the radio or glimpse a hitchhiker standing near the on-ramp of the freeway, and that will send my thoughts backward in time. By the age of twenty-two, after spending my summers hitchhiking, I had been through every one of the United States, traveling more than 50,000 miles. Doing this was, I suppose, a rite of passage for me.

I made up my own set of rules for hitchhiking: kept my hair short, never let myself get scruffy. I wouldn't stick out my thumb either. I took the cardboard out of shirts from the laundry and with a Magic Marker wrote the name of the town I wanted to go to in big block letters; then I'd stand where traffic was slow and the drivers could get a good look at me.

On the edges of small towns, cars filled with high-school girls would sometimes stop for me. Giggling softly, they would drive me slowly down their main street to the other side of town without ever saying a word.

Once, I remember, I was given a ride by the mayor of a town; a couple of times chauffeur-driven limousines stopped for me; the police picked me up sometimes and I'd spend the night on a cot in jail—they didn't book me or anything, it was just a free night's lodging. Occasionally itinerant families of farm workers would sandwich me in the back seat with their children.

But mostly I was given rides by men traveling alone— servicemen or salesmen in beat-up Chevys and Plymouths, truck drivers. They just wanted the company, and I was certainly nonthreatening. Riding beside them gave me my first lesson in how different the parameters that define a life can be.

When I asked these men what they did for a living, a lot of them would answer, disparagingly at first, "Well, I'm just a truck farmer," or "I'm just a salesman." But I was so eager to know what it meant to have a profession, I pressed them to tell me more about the work they did, and most of them would do so, sometimes growing animated when they saw how interested I was.

But some of the men who gave me rides wouldn't talk about themselves at all—except to say they wished they were young again, and that they would do things differently if they were starting out fresh. Their tired smiles of farewell when they let me out at a crossroads were almost like admonitions not to find myself, at middle age, wishing I'd done things differently.

Of course, I don't always think about the past during my buffer time on the freeways. Sometimes I plan trips or outings with my children, or changes at the hospital, many things, and I'm always grateful for this special, quiet time because I know I couldn't step out the front door of my house right into the white corridor.

6:58 A.M.—I exit the freeway, drive the few blocks along Beacon Street to the hospital, turn into the parking lot, and insert my card into the slot box. The gate rises. I park my car, lock the doors, and, as I walk toward the hospital, wonder if I am being watched by the security guards whose TV monitors observe the entrances and corridors of the hospital. The twentieth century has ushered in so many mechanical ways to invade our privacy, you'd think we'd all get used to it, but I never have.

Night is when the camera eye is trained on the parking lot, especially Saturday nights, or nights following the day that welfare checks have been received. That's when cars are broken into, windshields smashed, stereos stolen, tires slashed by people who've spent their money on highs that didn't last long enough.

Leaving the hospital on such nights, I feel the same skittery sensation at the back of my neck I felt in Ethiopia when I listened to the lions roaring inside their cages just a short distance up the road from where I lived. About thirty were kept confined near Emperor Haile Selassie's palace, and at night their voices seemed to grow louder. Or maybe their frustration at being caged became greater. I never knew, but there is something about darkness that makes the senses, the feelings, everything more acute.

Right now, however, the sun is shining. A wind from the canyons is even blowing the smog away from the city's horizon, and as I approach the hospital I wonder if any patients are left over from the night before.

I'll be taking over from Sy, who worked last night. He recently decided to do a residency in ENT (ear, nose, and throat) at another hospital, so he spends a lot of his daytime hours there, while still working the night shift in ER at Los Angeles Memorial.

Since my divorce, Sy and I have started taking in an occasional movie together or going out to dinner or sometimes just sitting in each other's living rooms and talking. Our friendship has reached the point where we can discuss some fairly serious questions. I asked him recently why, out of all the ER doctors here, he's never married.

"Look," he told me, "I'm a little overextended as it is, don't you think?"

That hit home, and I changed the subject.

7:05 A.M.—I walk through the ambulance entrance, turning into the first doorway on my left into the doctors' room. My desk is here, and an old swivel chair with the stuffing coming out of an inch-long rip in the seat. I suppose I could requisition a new chair, but my body has grown used to the contour of this one, depending on its familiar comfort. There is a filing cabinet next to the desk; a large bulletin board on the wall with the doctors' work schedule posted on it; bookshelves filled with medical texts; and a television set, mounted in one corner up near the ceiling, that's often on even when there's no one there to watch it. There's also a couch on which to catch forty winks if you have a quiet shift (I've been at Los Angeles Memorial for four years, and I haven't napped on that couch yet). Opposite the couch, running the length of the wall, is a closet full of white knee-length coats and green scrub suits.

I check my desk for messages, eye a folded copy of the

Los Angeles Times on top of the file cabinet, hoping I can read a little, then go into the bathroom, wash my hands, and come out ready to suit up.

Sy enters, sits down in the swivel chair, and props his feet on the desk. Sy has a high, bony forehead, gray eyes that seem always to be weighing, questioning, examining. He gestures now toward the bulletin board, and asks, "You ever look at that work schedule?"

I continue to suit up. "Levine, I make the thing out."

He picks up a pencil, stands, and draws check marks by eight of the eleven names on the schedule.

"Divorced," he says. "Eight out of eleven. Roughly seventy-three percent."

What brought this on? I look at him, wondering where this is leading. Then I glance at the chart; 73 percent is a pretty dismal ratio. "Well, some of them have remarried, and they seem to be doing okay," I say half-defensively.

"Oh, sure," he agrees. "Malone's on his third. The guy is also getting crisp around the edges . . . rubbing some of the wrong people the wrong way, in case you hadn't noticed."

I've noticed, all right, but I don't want to talk about it just now. Malone will be coming in at one o'clock today to work the relief shift with me, and I'll be able to watch him then, see what shape he's in.

Sy realizes I'm not going to discuss Malone, and stretches. "You going to make it tonight?" He starts taking off his white coat.

"Tonight?"

"Russo's at seven-thirty."

I had forgotten. But I don't have anything else planned, so I nod and say, "Sure." The wry look he gives me tells me he knows I forgot, but that it's all right.

"Anything left out there?" I ask.

"Not much. An attempted suicide we kept for observation. Oh, and Walrus."

"I didn't hear the old guy when I came in," I say.

"He fell asleep about an hour ago."

Walrus is one of our steadiest customers. He's been making regular visits to the emergency room since before I started at Los Angeles Memorial.

Sy stuffs his white coat and scrub suit in the bin and takes his sport coat out of the closet.

"Don't drop any," he says, then gives me a brief wave and leaves.

7:15 A.M.—I step out of the doctors' room. Midway down the corridor, seated in the alcove of the nurses' station—a long countertop with several swivel chairs pulled up to it—Calvin Bixby is drinking coffee and eating a doughnut so fresh the jelly oozes down his fingers, which means somebody made a doughnut run not too long ago.

Calvin is from Rhode Island, and looks like it; he has sharply delineated Yankee features, keen blue eyes. His job is meticulous, detail-oriented. He keeps track of all the paperwork the ER generates, hand-carries specimens to the lab on the days we're without volunteers, labels our blood samples and keeps them on ice until they can be taken to the lab, spends a lot of time on the phone trying to get test results from the technicians upstairs. As he puts it, "I live half my life on 'hold.'" Yet he somehow manages to maintain the same calm outlook (laced with dark humor) in the midst of crisis situations that he does when everything is quiet and running smoothly.

I look around for but don't see the doughnut box anywhere. Maybe it's in the nurses' lounge. I hope there's at least one left. That coffee and toast I had an hour ago are definitely not going to get me through the morning.

I glance at the patient chart rack on the left-hand wall of the nurses' station. Yellow stickers on the charts signify patients who are waiting to be seen by the floor nurses who will help them get undressed and into hospital gowns, monitor their vital signs, and elicit information about their complaints. Blue stickers mark the charts of patients ready to be seen by a doctor; green, patients waiting to be admitted into the hospital; brown, patients ready to be transferred to County. A red dot next to any sticker indicates a victim of an industrial accident. We try to see industrial-accident victims as quickly as we can, because often their injuries are minor and they are anxious to get back to work.

These color-coding stickers are put on the charts by the triage nurse, who occupies a small cubicle out in the waiting room. Triage comes from the French word *trier,* meaning to pick and assort according to quality. The term came to have medical significance during World War I, when soldiers needing treatment were screened according to their military value. Those who could be treated and returned to the front were seen before those who were too critically injured to be salvaged for fighting.

Here, the triage nurse decides in what order the people who have come to be admitted to the emergency room will be examined. If a person comes in with a minor problem, the nurse will send that person directly to the admitting clerk, who will type up the necessary forms for admittance to ER. But if someone walks in off the street and says they've been stabbed (which happens fairly frequently), and they remove the hand clutching their abdomen to reveal a gaping wound, the triage nurse will bring them back to ER to be seen immediately.

The ER nurses take turns rotating four-hour shifts at the triage desk. On a disaster-filled day the job can be arduous. Sometimes patients occupy every couch and chair in the waiting room while the relatives or friends who accompanied them lean tiredly against the wall or pace up and down the narrow spaces between the rows of chairs. Tempers rise to the snapping point then; fistfights have broken out when someone has left a chair for a moment and returned to find it occupied. The triage nurse will keep the door to the small office firmly shut at such times.

This morning Eugene is the triage nurse. Eugene is given the least-busy hours on the triage desk as often as possible, because he is the most prone to say about some of the patients who come to the emergency room, "These people don't belong here. They're not emergencies."

If you were to ask him who doesn't belong here, he would have no trouble telling you: patients who come in because they can't sleep; patients who ask for nonemergency prescriptions and refills; patients who bring on their own illnesses through drug or alcohol abuse, smoking, failure to observe basic safety precautions, or failure to comply with treatment prescribed by their physicians; patients who make multiple visits for the same old chronic complaint.

That would let Walrus out.

In fact, sometimes Eugene's characterization of non-emergencies would empty our treatment rooms.

Yet fortunately and surprisingly, Eugene's attitude doesn't affect his nursing. He's a good nurse—meticulous, thorough, and reliable. But his constant verbal animosity can get wearing. "The nice thing about Eugene," Calvin Bixby has said, "is how he can cheer you up just by going home."

I take the two charts out of the rack, Walrus's and the

attempted suicide's. Calvin looks up and says, "After everybody else checked out, I kept hoping they'd strike up a friendly conversation. You know, the way people do in a doctor's waiting room—'I'll tell you about my emphysema if you tell me why you tried to pop off.' But no such luck."

I glance through the glass partition into the main treatment room. Beds 1 through 5 are there, each equipped with an EKG monitor that can be connected to a monitor at the nurses' station.

The woman who attempted suicide is in bed 5. Alfred is taking her pulse. Alfred is from Oakland. He served as a nurse in a MASH unit during the Vietnam war. He is a small man, light and quiet on his feet. His skin is such a sooty black, if you walk with him out into the parking lot at night, his face almost disappears. Never have I seen him ruffled, nor do I expect to. As Calvin puts it, "We get down to maybe the fifth circle of hell here on occasion. But Alfred's seen the seventh."

At the far end of the room on bed 2, Walrus is sound asleep and snoring. Years ago I think the man must have been formidable. He isn't tall, probably not over five feet eight inches or so—but everything about him is large. His head is large; so are his ears; the breadth of his chest is massive. His forearms look more like thighs, and his feet are so huge they remind me of a clown's.

He has told us so many stories about himself, I feel I know him better than I do some of my relatives.

"Once," he said, "I worked the docks at San Pedro. Always got picked first. Could lift my weight in buffalos in those days.

"Another time," I heard him tell Illana, "I used to have my own fishing boat—ran her out of Anacortes up in Washington. Had me the prettiest Haida Indian girl you ever saw for my wife, and three fine sons, too. They're all gone now. The wife went first. Then the Korean war took two of the boys. The last one rode his motorcycle off a cliff . . ."

I don't know when we first started calling him Walrus, or who christened him that, though I suspect Calvin Bixby. I can picture Calvin seated at his desk at three in the morning, watching Phil—that's Walrus's real name, Phil—come lumbering down the corridor on his outsized feet, and I can hear Calvin saying, "Good God, it's the Walrus again."

The old man's emphysema seems to hit him the worst about three o'clock in the morning. When Walrus has trouble breathing, he gets scared. He lives in a hotel for transients a few blocks away, but there's no one there to give a damn whether he's breathing or not, so he comes to us. Unfortunately, by the time he gets here he's in a state of panic, which makes his breathing even more difficult and our job twice as hard.

Normal breathing is quiet, with a ratio of 2 to 1—breathing in lasts twice as long as breathing out. For people suffering from emphysema, asthma, bronchitis—or any debilitating lung condition—that ratio is reversed. Breathing out lasts twice as long as breathing in, because the alveoli, the thin-walled air sacs of the lungs where the exchange of oxygen and carbon dioxide takes place, are in spasm. The patient tries to force the air out; that can then result in wheezing, the worst of which turns into a thin rasp.

By the time Walrus gets to us, he's wheezing and rasping, convinced that this time he really is dying. We give him oxygen, which helps. The nurses work with him, using IPPB (intermittent positive pressure breathing), which also gives him some relief. But I sometimes wonder if it isn't being with people who are willing to watch over him that does the most good.

Walrus lumps Sy, the other ER doctors, and me together and calls us all Doc. The nurses he individuates by name: Pearl, Barbara, Illana, Alfred. He doesn't like Eugene, so he just calls him "you."

I wish, considering the sector of life he's in and the reasons he comes to us, that I could say we have grown fond of him. We haven't. Illana, Pearl, and Barbara have outmaneuvered his grasping hands too many times. We've heard his repertoire of stories too often, witnessed his panics over and over. "The next time Walrus comes in," Calvin Bixby vows, "I swear I'm going to boot him over to County."

It is a threat that can arouse panic in a lot of the people we see. Due to the volume of patients they see at County—they have 2000 beds—the body can only be viewed as a machine whose parts are there to be fixed. For people living on the edge, this can be the final straw in a long process of dehumanization.

Calvin won't send Walrus to County. Walrus is indigent and we're directed by our administration to send non-critical indigent patients to County so when paying patients walk in, we'll have beds for them.

Maybe Walrus knows this. Maybe that's why he always comes in around three o'clock in the morning—when we're most apt to have empty beds, and time. He's almost taken on the persona of an ailing troublesome relative we tolerate out of some dim sense of obligation.

We'll bed him down as we always do. We'll listen to Eugene's loud complaints about him as we always do. The nurses will undress him, holding his socks gingerly between thumb and forefinger, grimacing at the incredible aroma that emanates from between his toes. Whichever doctor is available will examine him, tell him to calm down and try to relax, and administer oxygen or an HHN (hand-held nebulizer); and then we will all listen to his lamentations (did I mention he also has a giant voice?) for the three or four hours it takes him to finally fall asleep.

We have a number of patients like Walrus, people with chronic diseases who have nowhere else to go and who see the ER as a kind of way station. I suppose we're the closest thing to a family they have.

And perhaps, to many of us, they raise the question: How far do any of us live, really, from the edge?

7:23 A.M.—I go into the main treatment room to see the attempted suicide. Her name, I read from her chart, is Lucy Wheeler.

Sitting upright on the bed, she is so thin her shoulder blades are visible beneath the hospital gown. Alfred is busy taking her blood pressure.

Bitter lines enclose her mouth—evidence, I think, of resentment and perhaps self-hate. Lucy's teal-blue eyes are wary and grim.

As I read her chart, Alfred pulls the screening curtain around her bed. Then he stands there, plumping the woman's pillows, straightening her sheets, and hovering beside her. What, I wonder, is going on? Alfred is always conscientious, but now his attitude seems almost parental.

Sy's notes from the night before tell me Lucy is thirty-three years old. Epileptic. She drank a large amount of vodka, then overdosed on sleeping pills. At some point during her suicide attempt, she pushed over a lamp in her apartment, and her landlady, hearing the crash, became suspicious and knocked on her door. When there was no answer she unlocked it, found Lucy, and summoned the paramedics.

Over my years in ER I've become aware of statistics on suicides. Although the suicide-attempt rate among women is double that among men, men succeed twice as often because they're more certain about wanting to die when they're in a suicidal crisis. Most men shoot themselves, with barbiturates being their second choice and hanging their third. Among women, barbiturates is the first choice, gunshot the second, and carbon monoxide the third. Some women seem to plan their suicides so that they will be found by family members or friends before it's too late. Most men do not.

I've never known what to say to attempted suicides, probably because I can't understand the impulse to destroy life. However, in this case I don't have to say anything. When Sy admitted her last night, he contacted one of the psychiatrists on staff. The psychiatrist expressed the opinion that her suicide attempt was probably due to a depressed mood triggered by the interaction of her seizure medication with alcohol; and that if she seemed okay throughout the night, to release her in the morning.

Sy, of course, had the option of informing the police we had an attempted suicide. But the police don't like it when we do that; in a city like Los Angeles, attempted suicides are way down on their list of priorities.

Of course if we have a suicidal patient who is also violent and/or irrational, we do call the police; they institute a 51/50, a 72-hour hold and transport the patient to the psych ward at County. It's a locked ward, and for a person who is still capable of reason, a 72-hour stay there can be a shattering experience.

Sy chose not to call the police. Studying Lucy, I don't think I would have either. All I really need to do now is sign the chart and release her.

That's what she obviously wants me to do. The teal eyes watch me with sharp anticipation, as though I were the warden of her prison.

"Is there someone we can call?" I ask. "Anyone who can come and take you home?"

She murmurs sullenly, "No one." If I had other patients to see, I wouldn't have the time to respond, but this morning there is no one else waiting, and I am curious about Alfred's protective attitude. So I sit on the edge of the bed and say, "Lucy, how long has it been since you've had the medication for your seizures checked?"

The blue eyes meet mine for a second before she turns away. "None of that stuff helps me."

I had already suspected that this was the problem, because I've seen other people whose seizures cannot be controlled by medication. They have a particular look about them, at once vulnerable and defiant. I think the vulnerability must come from never knowing when they will be stricken, when segments of their lives will disappear without a trace; and they are defiant from having to pretend this doesn't matter. The only thing that helps is access to people who care about them. I doubt Lucy has anyone who cares about her. Her alcoholism has probably driven everyone away.

Outside the curtain, I see Illana's gleaming white oxfords approach. "Dr. Sword? I have a child in pediatrics who needs stitches."

"Okay," I answer.

The corners of Lucy's mouth move faintly. She's pleased I'm being called away. That will leave her free to go home to swallow more vodka and pills. Reluctantly I lift my pen to sign the chart, when Alfred says, "Ah— doctor?"

Both Lucy and I look at him. He has been so quiet, we had forgotten he was there. He says to me, "Can I talk to you for a minute?"

Alfred has one of the most soothing, mellifluous voices I have ever heard. But at this moment, it's strained. I step outside the curtain, and Alfred, following, beckons me out into the corridor.

He points to Lucy's chart. "Today's her birthday," he says. I glance at the birth date entered on the chart. He's right. But I don't know what he wants me to do with this information.

"I was thinking—well, maybe we could fix up a cake," he says.

"What?"

"The bakery's nearby," he continues, running his words together fast so I won't have a chance to interrupt him. "It wouldn't take a minute. I could slip out and get a cake, stick a few candles in it, you know, and—"

Though many situations are unprecedented in ER, this is certainly a first.

I am speechless.

"It can't hurt," he says. "Can it?"

Suddenly I realize he's right, and I nod. "Go get the cake, Alfred. But hurry up. I've got to release her soon." He grins, and it occurs to me that although I have seen Alfred smile before, I have never seen him grin.

7:44 A.M.—Alfred leaves as I go to the nurses' station, pick up the child's chart, and start down the corridor toward the pediatrics room.

Pediatrics is at the far end of the corridor, next to the

double doors that open into the waiting room and the hospital proper. A code lock was put on those double doors awhile ago after a man burst through them waving a gun and threatening to shoot us all if we didn't give him something for his headache. From ER, we can open the doors by pushing a button on the wall. On the waiting-room side, the doors can be opened by punching numbered buttons in a coded sequence only the staff is privy to.

Sometimes people in the waiting room who have been there for hours become angry about the fact that those doors are kept locked, and threaten to force their way into ER. Then the security guards who monitor the waiting room on closed-circuit TV will come out and try to calm them down. Lobo, a one-time tackle for the Chicago Bears who is six feet eight inches tall and weighs in at 280 pounds, generally doesn't have to do anything more than walk slowly through the room.

Big Tim, our ex-prizefighter, could probably do the same thing, but he likes to calm the patients down by chatting with them. "How come the children in this part of town are better looking than in any other part of town?" he'll ask the mothers. And he's especially good with older people.

Once in a while he'll come back to ER and tell us if someone is too close to the edge of panic for him to be able to handle the situation safely. Following Tim's advice, we've averted several crises by sending a nurse out to talk to a sick and terrified person or by bringing an anxious husband back to see his wife or a mother to sit with her child.

It's hard to judge which parents are going to be helpful in an emergency situation and which ones are going to make things worse. Some hospitals have a blanket rule: No parents allowed.

The nurses at Los Angeles Memorial deal with the situation according to which doctor is on duty. Some of us are more willing than others to have the parents present. I'm one of these.

So I'm not surprised when I enter the pediatrics room to see a woman sitting with the child. She has a wide, flat-boned face, russet skin. California Indian tribe, I think, maybe Modoc or Shasta. She looks displaced, worn out, by the city. I worked among the Pueblo Indians in New Mexico right after I graduated from medical school, and I came both to admire and to be frustrated by their stoicism.

The child, a boy about seven, is lying quietly on the treatment table. The woman is seated on a straight chair at the far side. Neither of them acknowledge my smile nor my "Good morning," and so I lay the chart down and begin to examine the boy.

The wound on the upper left side of his forehead is perhaps half an inch long, and deep. Like all head wounds, it has bled profusely. Dried blood is caked over his face, a dark crust against the brown of his skin.

I examine, then begin to wash the wound. He winces, but tolerates it.

"He's going to need some stitches," I say to the mother.

She nods.

As I work on her son I ask the woman, "How did it happen?"

Her reply is curt. "A rock fight."

I sense she respects the white coat and instruments, but does not necessarily trust me. She watches my movements carefully.

"How long since he's had a tetanus shot?" I ask her.

She doesn't answer.

"Well, he'll have to have one," I say.

She nods impassively.

But the boy comes to life writhing like an eel. Had I been suturing his wound at that moment, I might have put my needle in his eye.

"No shot!" he yells. "No damn shot!"

I stopped fighting with children long ago, and am about to call a nurse and a volunteer to hold him down when suddenly the mother stands up beside me. I am six feet three; the top of her head doesn't even come to my shoulder, but when she says, "Jay, you shut your mouth," her authority far outreaches mine.

The boy grows quiet, but his black eyes flash from her face to mine, and as I give him the shot I wonder if he is angrier at her, for putting him in the hands of a stranger, or at me, for inflicting pain. No matter. Her expression doesn't change at all.

I continue working on the boy, and when it is time for me to inject Novocaine into the lips of the wound I summon Illana and Dennis to hold him.

Tall and willowy slim, Illana enters the room purposefully. Long before she came to Los Angeles Memorial she mastered the art of instilling confidence in patients with her "let's-get-on-with-it" attitude. Born in Jamaica, she worked in hospitals in New Orleans, Chicago, and Detroit before coming to the West Coast. Her years in the United States haven't taken away the lilting West Indies rhythms of her speech, and this softens her brisk professionalism. For the last four years, she's been living with a policeman named Joe.

Dennis is a premed student from Loyola who donates his time here on Tuesdays and Wednesdays. His approach to the treatment table where Illana and I wait for him is tentative. He wants to be helpful; he's just never absolutely sure that he will be.

"This is going to sting for a minute," I tell the child, meaning the words for the mother as well. I want her to know he has the right to yell now if he wants to, because I have to inject that Novocaine needle in several places around the edges of the wound to anesthetize the area.

The kid screams like holy hell and twists and pulls so hard that Dennis grunts twice and I see the muscles flexed in Illana's forearms. The boy does succeed in freeing one hand, his fingers grabbing for the needle. Instantly his mother reaches out, grips that hand, holds on. Not until I announce to the room at large, "It isn't going to hurt any more," does she let go.

I put in eight stitches, then tell the kid he can sit up. He eyes me sullenly as he does, but when I show him his stitches in the small hand mirror, he's interested. Then Dennis makes him a balloon. To make a balloon in the emergency room, we blow up one of the thin-skinned gloves we wear. Inflated, the five fingers look like spiky hair. The part that encases the palm becomes the head. Dennis paints a face on it with marking pens and presents it to the child: black eyes, red mouth, with a row of stars on the forehead to mark the battle scar.

I expect no response from either the boy or his mother, but the child surprises me with a sudden smile. "It's me," he says.

8:11 A.M.—I go out into the corridor to watch Alfred un-box Lucy's birthday cake at the nurses' station and then stick some candles in the center. If Eugene were back here with us instead of up at the triage desk, I think for once events would render him speechless. Even Calvin Bixby, when he sees the cake and asks what's going on (and we tell him), says he will not participate.

But five minutes or so later when Alfred, Illana, Dennis, and I are standing at the foot of Lucy's bed, Calvin comes in to watch. Alfred places the pink-and-white cake on a portable table next to Lucy, and is definitely in charge of the occasion as he begins to light the candles.

Amazement nearly gives way to panic on Lucy's face as she stares at the cake, then at him, and us. I think she is terrified by this kind of attention, especially from strangers.

"Now," Alfred says, "we're going to do this a little differently than usual. Each one of us will make a wish for you on your candles—not out loud, just to ourselves. When we've finished, you can make one too, if you feel like it."

He turns to Illana, gesturing for her to step forward. She does so matter-of-factly, her poise certainly a contrast to my self-consciousness.

She remains by the cake only a few seconds before resuming her position at the foot of the bed.

A few seconds later, after Dennis and Alfred, my own turn comes. I start to step forward, but it's Calvin Bixby who moves toward the cake. To my surprise he speaks softly to Lucy, saying, "Hey . . . we just wanted you to know that none of us ever expect to see you back here again—not even for another cake."

I think Lucy is struggling with hysteria. She looks as though something is going to break loose at any minute. Then Alfred says, "You can blow out the candles now."

She quickly leans forward and blows them out, forgetting about making a wish herself, or maybe she never intended to. A few minutes later, I sign her chart, and after Illana helps her dress, Lucy leaves the hospital carrying her cake. As I watch her walk down the corridor, I wonder what memories she awakened in Alfred.

We all carry memories around with us, even Eugene. They cause intense and unexpected reactions to certain patients who echo fears and frustrations buried inside us. Quite often we don't realize what's happening at the time; only later do we make a connection.

9:57 A.M.—When I step out into the corridor again, I see Illana sliding a chart marked with a red dot and a blue sticker into the rack. She tells me an industrial-accident victim is waiting in the suturing room.

I pick up the chart and walk down the corridor, and when I enter I see a woman my Germantown, Pennsylvania, grandfather might have called "comely." She has expressive, intelligent gray eyes, a delicate mouth.

As I look at her, the section of my brain that calculates age comes up with thirty-seven. But when I glance at the birth date entered on her chart, I discover she is twenty-five.

The tip of her little finger has been severed.

"How did this happen?" I ask.

She tells me she is an assembly-line worker in a toy factory, where her job is to drill armholes in doll bodies. On this particular morning, she must not have been paying close attention to what she was doing, because, as she puts it, "The drill finally got me."

The phrase has a certain resonance, and I wonder if every morning she gets up and goes to work feeling that the sharp bit of the drill is lying in wait, ready for the smallest lapse in her attention.

"Your injury's not serious," I tell her. "You'll be able to go back to work in a week."

She glances past me, nodding, expressionless. A minute earlier (when I was only half listening) she'd mentioned her three small children; evidently she is their only support. As I finish bandaging her finger, I ask her if her children are in school, and she begins to chat about them. She smiles as she describes her oldest boy's artistic talent: "It's just terrific how he can draw, doctor, especially faces. Real hard stuff, you know?" Her smile brightens. "For Christmas he drew my portrait—it's better than a photograph. Kids are amazing, huh?"

I return her smile. "I know. I have three of my own."

"You do? How old?"

A bond of communication is formed for a few moments, even though she and I are opposites in so many ways. She loathes her job but has a close relationship with her children; my own work overwhelms me until sometimes my son and daughters seem like mirages. But for a brief time the factory she works in and my problems vanish as we talk softly, exchanging anecdotes about our children.

When I have finished bandaging her finger and leave the treatment room, I am thinking—as I so often do in this hospital—about fortune, the options some of us are offered and others simply aren't.

While I was in medical school, I worked for the Job Corps for Women, a government-funded program (long since plowed under) that focused on teaching new job skills to women who were struggling with poverty. I'll never forget the expressions I saw on the faces of some of those women when they perceived there might be a way to change their lives.

And I remember, of course, how badly I once wanted to change mine.

At age eighteen, I felt caught in a lock-step pattern. I wanted to go to college, or I thought I did, if only because that's what young males of my background did in the early 60s. Because of my father's recent death, I didn't feel I should live away from home. And my mother's financial resources were restricted. I hadn't made good enough grades in high school to be accepted at the University of Pennsylvania (I had high grades in my science classes, but mediocre grades in everything else). However, there was a specialized college near my home, the Philadelphia College of Textile Science, where I could enroll, so that's what I did.

For almost four years I labored toward a degree in textile science until there came a day in my senior year when—as I stood in a room filled with bubbling vats of dye—my head began to spin with nausea, and I realized I'd spent the last four years learning how to be something I didn't want to be. And I remembered the sad eyes of those men who had picked me up when I was hitchhiking, the ones who wished they had done things differently, who saw their lives as treadmills.

I graduated from the textile college, but I didn't take any of the jobs that were offered to me. Instead, I began to look for a way out. I could, I discovered, become a Navy pilot at the Flight Training School at Pensacola (which would entail a five-year commitment from me).

Or I could join the Peace Corps (a two-year commitment).

In fact, the timing of events was such that I could go to California, take my Peace Corps training at UCLA, and if it turned out I wasn't suited to the Corps, I could report to Pensacola in the fall.

Life doesn't get much more generous than that.

As soon as I arrived in California, the idea of becoming a pilot disappeared. It wasn't just the mystique Los Angeles held for an inland-bred Easterner. I found myself living in a brand-new milieu. My fellow Peace Corps volunteers were almost all liberal-arts majors—burgeoning artists, writers, philosophers, teachers. They would sometimes stay up until dawn discussing philosophical questions in a way that I had never heard. At first I just listened, but gradually I began to join in.

And day by day in California I grew more determined that the second chance life was giving me would not be wasted.

9:48 A.M.—Alfred tells me he has just taken the vitals of a thirteen-year-old girl in the main treatment room who has abdominal pain and looks sick. When Alfred uses the word "sick," it's like a red flag. I pick up the patient's chart and go on in.

The girl is big-boned and plump, with skin a charcoal color that looks as if it has been lightly dusted with talc. I lift up the hospital gown to probe her abdomen. Her eyes are closed, but she is too tense for sleep, and when I touch her she moans and pushes my hand away. Her temperature is 104.

The girl's father is seated on the straight metal chair beside the bed. He is wooden and silent, almost hostile, as I examine his daughter, and suddenly I feel an uncomfortable sensation in the pit of my stomach. I've felt it before, and I know why it happens.

When I worked in the hospital in Redondo Beach, a lot of my patients were among that middle-class suburban population I call "the worried well," people who weren't terribly sick, only worried that they might be. They talked to me freely about the things that were troubling them. But here in downtown Los Angeles, the people who drag themselves into the emergency room hoping they're not really sick, often are. They can't afford sickness, either for themselves or their families, and they don't want to talk to me about being sick.

This wrenching feeling I get in the pit of my stomach every now and then happens when I'm hoping someone here will look at me openly and accept what I have to offer—or at least not immediately put up a wall of resistance.

"How long has she been running a fever?" I ask the father.

A shrug. "Maybe three, four days."

"You don't know how long your own daughter's been sick?" I snap. I'm suddenly so irritable you'd think I was at the end of my shift, and I tell myself to lighten up.

"I drive a delivery truck," the man responds. "Leave the house at dawn and get home late. I don't know if Nell's been running a fever when I'm gone. Ain't nobody can stay home with her. I know she don't go to school. She's sick, that's all. Today's my day off, so I bring her in."

Regret washes over me for having been abrupt with this man. The girl's abdomen is so tender, she flinches every place I touch her. There is costovertebral tenderness when my fingers approach a spot below the ribs where the kidneys are.

"Has she been vomiting?" I ask.

"I think she did once, maybe."

"Does she have to urinate frequently?"

"I don't know."

I try to get the girl to answer me. "Nell, do you have to go to the bathroom more than usual? Does it hurt when you urinate?"

Silence.

"Do you have back pain?"

Still silence.

"I know you're not asleep. Answer me."

Nothing.

I rub her sternum sharply with my knuckle. "Answer me, Nell."

A moan, and then, "Yes! Lemmme alone."

I look up. The father's gaze is cold.

I tell him, "I think she has pylonephritis, which is a kidney infection. I'm going to order a urinalysis and a blood test. If the results confirm the infection, I'll ask a pediatrician from the hospital to come down and look at her. She needs to be admitted."

"How much is it going to cost?" he asks.

I shake my head. "I don't know."

The girl continues to feign sleep. I leave them, and I am mantled in gloom, weary of stoicism, weary of the pestilence of poverty.

"It's changing you," Sandy asserted when our marriage was disintegrating. "The things you see day after day are changing you. You walk in this house and it's an hour before you can even see *us*."

Sometimes I do sense something eroding inside me. And yet I know if I become desensitized to my patients and their problems, I will no longer do my job well.

I go back out to the nurses' station, write the orders for the CBC (complete blood count) and the urinalysis on the girl's chart, and hand it to Calvin Bixby. "Use your influence to speed up the results on these, will you?"

"Influence? Oh, certainly," he says drily.

Then he eyes me shrewdly. "You look like maybe you could use something more than my influence. Anything wrong?"

I shrug. "No, I'm okay."

"You sure?"

"Yeah. I don't suppose you know what happened to the doughnut box?"

He shakes his head, rummaging through the pile of paperwork on his desk.

"Got something for me?" I ask.

"Yeah, a cop came in a few minutes ago with a baby. He's waiting for you to do a well-child exam so he can take the baby over to Sitton."

Sitton is L.A.'s custodial-care home for abandoned, abused, and neglected children.

Calvin finds what he's looking for, the physical examination form used by the County, and hands it to me, and I head once more down the white corridor.

10:12 A.M.—The policeman is standing next to the small crib bed where the infant is lying, but my eyes are drawn at once to the opposite side of the room, where a woman is leaning against the wall.

Calvin didn't mention that the mother was still with the child. I have to assume, since her baby is being taken to Sitton, that she is in custody. The woman looks half starved. Her flat-breasted body reminds me of a child's, but her pinched, heart-shaped face is old. She is one of those people I see occasionally whose ethnogeny is blurred by the mingling of several races. Some of these people are hauntingly beautiful. I think she may have been once. Her hair, the texture of lamb's wool, is dyed a bright persimmon orange. Her skin is caramel-colored. The eyes, faintly slanted, are a clear green.

When the cop sees me standing in the doorway, he tells her, "Take the baby's clothes off so the doctor can examine him." She doesn't react or acknowledge that she has heard him. I enter the room, conscious of the hostility that is like a laser beam connecting these two.

"It's okay," I say, moving toward the bed. "I'll undress the child." I wonder how many hours they've been together, this woman and the policeman, and what it is in each that has so alienated the other.

The cop seeks me as an ally at once. "Would you look at this? One lousy diaper, a T-shirt! That's all the frigging clothes she has for him."

I'm startled by his anger.

"What you have to look at my kid for?" the woman asks suddenly. But those green eyes aren't focused on me, they're watching the cop. And I can tell she doesn't really expect an answer to her question. The words are calculated to needle him. She digs further. "Why are you taking away my kid? I ain't done nothing to him. I give him some titty every day." She begins to smile. "Sweet and fresh, just how he likes it. You come on home with me, honey, and I'll do the same for you."

She does draw blood.

"Fucking bitch," the cop retorts, then quickly turns away.

The crease in his pants has an edge to it. His hair is well groomed, and the black shoes gleam with polish. The man obviously takes pride in what he is. Yet with scarcely any effort at all, this woman has elicited a breach in his professionalism.

A moment later, however, the woman stops being aware of either one of us or of her child. With delicate finger movements, she begins to pluck at the air, as if there were thistle tops floating down from the ceiling. And I see the tracks on her forearms. The cop watches her briefly before turning back to the child. I turn too. The infant has a beautifully modeled head with a soft tangle of dark hair. But even as I look at him, a fit of tremors causes those fragile bones to quiver.

There is no birth date given on the physical examination chart I am to fill in, but the baby can't be more than a month old. When I touch him he begins to cry. It's piercing, high-pitched, the kind of sound a person can't listen to very long. I feel the child's bones, palpate his abdomen, probe his scrotum. The boy is healthy in all ways but one: he is addicted to heroin. Between 2 and 5 percent of babies born in urban areas today are addicted to some drug. Before treatment, the death rate is 20 to 50 percent; after treatment, 3 to 30 percent. Most never make it to the hospital.

Is this why the cop hates the woman so much, because she has inflicted her addiction on her child? Yet he must have seen far worse—children beaten to death, for instance. Does he have a bitter memory, perhaps, of another addict, maybe someone he knew, someone close to him, and the frustration, the failure still haunt him?

I diaper the baby with a clean hospital diaper. I'll have to get him admitted to pediatrics. The mother is still plucking delicately at the air as I leave the room. Tomorrow, will she miss her child? Or even remember he's gone? I do know this. The policeman will remember everything.

10:47 A.M.—Dr. Jim Blandsford accosts me as I enter the corridor. Jim is a gnome of a man with prominent ears and a long beard that comes to a point.

He puts in a long day. He's a pediatrician who specializes in oncology, so a lot of his patients are children with cancer.

"Sword," he says to me now, "that's a sick girl in there."

He's talking about Nell.

"Are you going to admit her?" I ask.

"Yep. I'm probably going to have to throw every antibiotic I can at her."

"She should have been brought in sooner," I say glumly.

He's writing on her chart. "Well, it's lucky she was brought in at all." Then he glances up at me. "You okay?"

I shrug. "End-of-the-month blahs is all. Listen, I need you to admit an infant I just looked at. He's been taken away from his mother; addicted to heroin."

Jim nods. "Sure. Hey, Carrie's coming in around six tonight. We're having a pizza party. Come on up if you're not bogged down here."

Carrie is Jim's girl friend, a grad student in theater arts at UCLA. She comes to Jim's pediatric ward about once a month and puts on a mime show for the children. She's good enough, for the time that she's there, to make the kids forget they're sick and hurting.

A lot of the kids Jim treats don't know whether they're ever going to get better. I've heard it said that some illnesses are ennobling. "Living candles" is a phrase I heard recently. People afflicted with grave debilitating illnesses supposedly become living candles, illuminating the lives of the rest of us. Do they? I'd certainly question it. All I know is I feel like crying when I see some of Jim's children.

"Okay," I tell him, "I'll come up if I have time."

He smiles. "Good. Pineapple and pepperoni on the pizza. The kids love it."

11:05 A.M.—I find the doughnut box at last—on a chair in the general examination room. This is where we see people we can't put in any specific category. Some of our most unusual patients have been treated in this room—the bag lady with hives, for example, who came in swathed in old brown newspapers. As I clipped them off her with a pair of surgical shears, I found myself reading a sports page to see how the Dodgers had done three years ago.

This is also where we have a refrigerator we try to keep stocked with orange juice and soft drinks. There isn't any orange juice now, but I'll settle for the doughnuts. I lift the lid and peer inside. Two halves are left. Half a maple bar, half a chocolate glazed. I carry them into the corridor to see if there's fresh coffee yet at the stand near the nurses' station.

Our volunteer, Dennis, is sitting there taking a break. He's an intense-looking young man, curly brown hair, skin remarkably pale for a Southern Californian—but then he spends most of his time indoors, either in the classroom, or studying, or volunteering here at the hospital. He's been kept busy this morning, carrying specimens to the lab for Calvin Bixby, changing sheets on the gurneys, helping with patients.

Dennis is doing something more than volunteering here, though. He is watching us and watching himself, too, asking, "Do I have it in me to become a doctor?" I wonder when it was that Dennis first discovered he wanted to become a physician.

Sy told me he thought *he* was born knowing it. He says he has an absolutely clear memory of reaching for the stethoscope that hung around the neck of the pediatrician his mother took him to when he was small, and of having it pried out of his hands. He also remembers screaming until his mother found him a facsimile in a toy store.

I didn't know I wanted to become a doctor until I was in my twenties. The seed may have been planted much earlier, but I didn't consciously acknowledge it until I went to Ethiopia with the Peace Corps. My assignment was to teach science at Tafari Makonnen, a high school run by Canadian Jesuits in Addis Abbaba. It was the only nongovernment high school in the country, and the most esteemed.

The academic day was rigorous. It started at 8:00 A.M. and ended at 6:00 P.M. The hours from 4:30 to 6:00 were a compulsory study hall for the students, since many students had no electricity in the houses inside the compounds where they lived. And a lot of them didn't have access to study time anyway once they left the school—they had too many chores to do.

Some of the students started first grade at Tafari Makonnen at age fifteen, because they had to be old enough to live on their own away from their families before they could enter. I taught biology and physics in the equivalent of our grades 8 through 12. I had thirty-six students in each of my seven classes, and some of them were older than I was. During the one recess, from 3:30 to 4:30, I was the basketball coach and scoutmaster.

The students were conscious of my vulnerability as a foreigner in Ethiopia and tried to protect me from anything they perceived as threatening to my well-being— partly, perhaps, because there were no substitutes in that school. If I didn't show up, my students would be sent to sit in a large hall monitored by men with whips, townsmen who took the job for the money and who would use the whips on recalcitrant boys because they knew they would lose their positions if they didn't.

I knew most of the students had come to Tafari Makonnen at great sacrifice to their families and that the education they were obtaining was vital to them. Teaching them, I felt totally needed. It was the first time in my life I had ever experienced feeling indispensable, and something in me responded immediately. My subconscious began to play with scenarios in which I could go on feeling that way, and it was then I began to grow increasingly aware of the cadre of young doctors who had come to Ethiopia.

The administrators of the Peace Corps, believing Americans sent to third world countries might contract exotic diseases, recruited doctors just out of medical school to accompany us—to take periodic blood and urine tests and just generally to keep tabs on our health.

Until then, the only physicians I'd ever had any contact with had been middle-aged men who intimidated me. When at fifteen my leg was broken in football practice, the surgeons who operated on it seemed cold, far more interested in the leg bone than the person it belonged to. And the doctors who tried to save my father were grim-faced, silent men (possibly because they were losing him). Somewhere along the way, too, I had been told (probably by my high-school Latin teacher, whose course I came close to flunking) that doctors, like priests, had to be fluent in Latin.

Yet here in Ethiopia, treating my dysentery, testing me for malaria, sharing tidbits of news from home, were young people not unlike myself. I found myself observing them during leisure hours on weekends—and in the evenings I'd lie awake on my cot listening to the clop-clop of camel hooves, or to the strange night howling of the hyenas, and I'd think about the young doctors.

Something was taking shape in my mind that came to fruition during my first summer vacation period.

We weren't allowed to return to the United States during the summer. As an integral part of our Peace Corps experience, we were expected to undertake a study project in the country to which we had been assigned. I chose to study public health. As a result, I was sent to visit almost every health facility in Addis Abbaba—the hospitals, the leprosarium, the TB sanitarium, the insane asylums. And my fascination with doctoring escalated.

A group of German surgeons who staffed a small hospital within easy walking distance of the compound where I lived encouraged me to watch the operations they performed. They couldn't have had a more rapt spectator. During surgery, they spoke German among themselves, but afterwards would answer my questions in English. And when the second teaching year began, I continued to visit that hospital at least once a week.

I was determined now to become a doctor.

However, I knew the odds were against me. The cutoff age for acceptance at most medical schools was twenty-six, and I was twenty-three, with almost a year of service still ahead of me in the Peace Corps. I had received good grades at the textile college, but that college had a specialized focus; I didn't know whether medical schools would look on my studies there as providing adequate preparatory work. And although I was teaching biology at Tafari Makonnen, I'd never taken college-level biology courses.

But I was obsessed. And being obsessed generally makes people difficult to live with, as Sandra has pointed out to me, but it also endows them with perseverance.

After school started, during the lunch hour while almost everyone else was napping (it was the hottest, sleepiest part of the day), I would go to the room where typing was taught, take down one of the typing manuals, and work on teaching myself to type. A revolving fan turned lazily above my head, and the sound the typewriter made seemed abnormally loud. I felt as if I were the only person moving in the whole school, but I persevered.

As soon as I could manage well enough, I obtained

the names and addresses of fifty medical schools in the midwestern and western United States and wrote each one a letter, telling them that my experiences in Ethiopia had convinced me I wanted to become a doctor, and asking if they would consider accepting me.

Thirty of my fifty letters went unanswered.

Approximately a dozen medical schools replied they weren't interested in me or my missionary zeal.

A half dozen or so responded, asking for more information, telling me I would probably have to enroll as a college freshman, and when I had completed four years, then they would evaluate me.

But five of the responses I received gave me hope, including one especially, from a Dean Willian Curran at the University of New Mexico. He suggested that I enroll there as a special student for a year—after which I would be evaluated. I knew that was the chance I had been hoping for, so at the end of my two years in the Peace Corps, I went to the University of New Mexico at Albuquerque.

Now, as I watch the young premed students like Dennis who volunteer at California General, and the emergency medicine residents at USC who come before me to take their boards, I can't help wondering what it was that started each of them toward medicine.

Dennis, I know, has doubts about himself. But I don't have doubts about Dennis. His hands never shake. His eye doesn't flinch from the sight of pain or blood. He asks intelligent questions. Dennis is going to be fine. But, of course, he is the one who has to discover that.

11:25 A.M.—I see Eugene talking on the biocom, which means Alfred is on the triage desk now.

Eugene's light-brown hair is beginning to recede and

thin, and he arranges it carefully to conceal this fact. He wears thick-lensed glasses to correct his nearsightedness and frequently experiments with different rims to see which ones will enhance the shape of his face. Today's are tortoise-shell and rest too low on the bridge of his nose. He replaces the receiver as I draw near and starts for the trauma room, telling me over his shoulder, "RAs are bringing in a shoot-by; leg wound."

My first gunshot victim today. Some shifts I make it through to noon without one.

A shoot-by occurs when someone in a moving car guns down a person standing on the street. The police tell me shoot-bys used to occur pretty much exclusively among rival gang members, but that in the past years, as unemployment among minorities has escalated, anyone on the street seems to be fair game.

The RA unit arrives without sirens, so the victim must have been picked up close to the hospital. They wheel him in, a tall, skinny blond kid lying on the gurney. He's wearing faded jeans, a yellow windbreaker. The paramedics guide the gurney into the trauma room, transfer the boy to the Stryker bed, place his belongings on the countertop, then hurry away to answer another call.

I examine the wound; it looks bad. I think the tibia may be shattered. The bone is close to the surface on the shin, and healing is always a problem here.

The medical form that was partially filled out in the rescue ambulance tells me the boy's name is Brian Warren; he's nineteen. He has brown eyes, and a light spattering of freckles across the bridge of his nose. His belongings on the countertop catch my eye. There's a duffel bag and a cowboy hat that once was white.

"Well, it looks like you ran into the bad guys," I say.

Somewhere he must have learned humor is an antidote to pain because he responds, "Yeah, right on the edge of town. That's where they got me."

"You don't live in L.A.?"

"Nope."

"Where're you from?"

"North." He winces.

"Where're you headed?"

"South."

I raise an eyebrow, and he comes as close as he can to grinning, considering the shape his leg is in. "I'm from Portland, Oregon. I've been hitchhiking, trying to get to San Diego so I can crew on *The Californian*."

"Tell me about it," I say. The way he said 'Californian' made it sound like something holy.

He's still in shock as he begins to talk, not yet realizing or feeling the full extent of damage to his leg.

"*The Californian* is a replica of an 1840 topsail schooner, the kind that used to chase smugglers and slave ships off the coast during the Gold Rush days. She's built out of long-leaf yellow pine, mahogany, and tropical hardwoods, just like ships were in the 1800s. She's being used to train sea cadets to sail ships the way they did a century ago. I've been dreaming about crewing on a ship like her ever since I was a little kid."

He hoists himself up on one elbow and asks me, "Have you ever seen a schooner with her sails unfurled?"

I shake my head.

Just then, the x-ray technician appears in the doorway, and I nod at her to come in. "Brian," I say, "I'll be back when your x-rays are finished."

Eugene accompanies me out into the corridor. I can tell from the look on his face he's prickling with outrage. "I don't care when they shoot their own," he says, "but a boy like that!"

I never know what to say to Eugene at such times.

I once heard Alfred trying to explain to Eugene what it can mean to be a member of a permanent underclass. "They don't perceive the sanctity of life, because theirs isn't sanctified. And they don't care if they get caught for shooting somebody, because any punishment they receive doesn't change their lives for the worse. Their lives are already worse."

But Eugene's reply was, "Anybody can change his life if he really wants to."

When the x-ray technician comes out of the trauma room, Eugene goes back in. I stand for a moment, leaning against the wall, remembering the twenty-nine days I spent in the hospital with my broken leg. My goal in life at that point was to make the varsity football lineup. My leg was shattered when I was tackled by a kid double my weight. I had to go into surgery three times for two closed and one open reduction; steel screws were inserted in my leg and it hurt like hell (it still hurts in damp weather or when I have to stand for long periods). But strangely enough, the tedium of having to lie in that hospital bed week after week is more vivid in my mind than the pain.

As I lay there, I acknowledged that I had never appreciated mobility before—and that there were far more important things than the varsity lineup. It was no coincidence, I'm sure, that when I went back to school my grades improved. Well, life had given me a little shake, which I needed. But I don't think Brian does. He seems to have his priorities well in hand.

When the technician brings me the x-rays, I pin them up on the light board at the nurses' station. It's just as bad as I suspected it would be. The bullet literally exploded the tibia. He's going to have problems with that leg for the rest of his life. Right now, he's in for a long hospital stay; and I don't see him climbing the riggings on any topsail schooner in the near future. Nor do I want to be the one to tell him that.

When I go back into the trauma room, a policeman is there trying to fill out the crime report, but he hasn't gotten very far.

"She's 90 feet long," Brian is saying, "and she has 14 ports of call."

He falls silent when he sees me holding his x-rays.

The policeman moves to one side of the bed while I tell Brian about the fracture and the long recovery period ahead. When I have finished, Brian doesn't speak for several moments.

Neither does anyone else.

"Well, maybe I can work on writing some of the coursework while I'm in bed," he says finally. "I mean, I might not be such a hot sailor for a while—but I can still teach. Nobody knows more about sailing a topsail schooner than I do. I've already memorized everything that's ever been written about them."

The corners of the policeman's mouth start to relax. Eugene clangs something softly against the side of the crash cart. It's going to take more than a shattered tibia to mess up Brian's dream.

11:47 A.M.—I see Illana wheeling Fareeba Sitani into the general examination room, with her brother Rashi slowly following. I've probably treated Fareeba half a dozen times in the past eighteen months. She and Rashi are students from Iraq, both pursuing degrees in international law.

Almost two years ago Fareeba's spinal cord was severed in an automobile accident, leaving her a paraplegic.

Since then she has had a recurring history of bladder infections necessitating—if her treating physician is unavailable—trips to the emergency room for irrigation of her bladder, injections of antibiotics, and recatheterization.

While Illana is getting her settled, Rashi asks if I have a few minutes to talk with him. It's quiet right now, so I say, "Yes, sure," and I take him into the doctors' room. Rashi sits on the chair beside the desk, picks up a pencil that is lying near the telephone, and begins rolling it between his fingers, saying finally, "I am not sure what I should do about Fareeba."

The last couple of times his sister has come to the emergency room I have sensed that her recurring infections must be at least partially due to her unwillingness to communicate her physical needs to her brother, and I suspect this is what Rashi wants to talk to me about. "Go on," I say.

"It is important that I do well in my studies, not only to me, but also to my family. Yet I am spending so much time worrying, my grades are suffering. I may not even be able to stay in school." His eyes meet mine, and I notice his color is not good. He's lost weight.

Again, I say, "Go on," only more softly.

"Arabian women are taught to be modest, you see— even with the male members of their families. Since the accident, in order for me to help her, Fareeba has had to allow me access to her physical person in ways that are demeaning to her. And when I should be able simply to approach and say 'How can I help you?' I must instead try to finds ways to circumvent her shame. This takes a great deal of time and energy. I wish I could tell you what I mean in my own language."

"You're doing all right in English," I say.

The Arabian eyes, dark, anxious, meet mine. "You understand?"

I nod.

"Can you tell me what to do?"

There aren't going to be any clear solutions for Rashi, or for Fareeba. I know relatives of accident victims are sometimes as decimated by tragedy as the victims themselves, and that has always troubled me.

"Can you tell Fareeba what you're telling me?" I ask.

"I don't think so. I've tried. Each morning when I wake up, I say to myself, today is the day I will tell her to stop hiding from me. But when I go to her room . . ." He shakes his head.

"Do you want me to talk to her?" I am a likely choice, I think, if only by virtue of the fact that I have no ongoing relationship with either of the Sitanis.

But Rashi shakes his head. "Her shame would be greater if she knew I was talking to you."

"Sometimes a little mortification is good for the soul," I respond. "Especially if something has to change."

"Well, but you can't obliterate centuries of tradition with a—a talk."

"No," I agree. "It takes a severed spinal cord to do that."

He doesn't reply.

"And what about Fareeba's studies?" I ask. "Is she doing well in school?"

"The past three quarters, she has gotten straight A's. But school is her whole life now."

"And is worrying about her going to be yours?"

He doesn't answer.

"I suppose you know worry is more destructive to concentration than pain," I continue, knowing I am prodding him; but I think someone has to, and he came to me.

He still doesn't answer.

"Look, can you afford to hire a nurse for her?"

"No."

"Is there any other member of your family who can come here and care for her?"

"No."

"Then what are your options?"

He replaces the pencil in the precise place where it was and stands up. "I thank you for taking the time to talk with me."

I walk with him as far as the corridor, remaining in the doorway of the doctors' room, watching him. He exchanges a few words with Illana, who then presses the button that opens the doors to the waiting room, and Rashi disappears.

Fareeba's chart has been placed in the rack, and I pick it up and thumb through it. It's a bulky chart, with a thick sheaf of pages chronicling her past visits. All I need to do, really, is examine her briefly, then initial the procedures Illana has written up.

But as I walk down the corridor toward the general examination room, my conversation with Rashi lingers in my mind. Fareeba, lying quietly on the bed, turns her head toward the doorway as I enter, and for the first time I notice her resemblance to her brother—especially the eyes.

"Well, I understand congratulations are in order," I say with a cheerfulness I don't feel.

"For what?" she asks.

"Pulling down a four-point-oh for three straight quarters." I begin to examine her.

She smiles slightly. "When I'm not in class, or sleeping, I'm studying."

"You're fortunate to be able to do that," I say. "Not many people can."

A tiny frown creases her forehead. I doubt anyone has told her since her accident that she is fortunate, and she doesn't like it.

In a few moments I finish the examination, then step back, uncertain of what I'm going to say, or even whether I should say anything at all. But I just can't believe this particular situation calls for two victims. I speak slowly, deliberately. "Fareeba, have you asked Rashi lately how he's doing with his studies?"

"Why?" Her tone is curt.

I don't back down. "Why not? I should think it would interest you."

She's on guard now. Her eyes are wary.

I continue, "His grades are falling, Fareeba. He may not even be able to stay in school."

Her voice rises. "Our grades are our concern, not yours. I don't know why he spoke to you at all. That was very wrong."

"No, it was right. Look, Fareeba, I'm already treating one Sitani. I don't want to have to treat another. Rashi's worrying himself sick over you and the fact that you won't let him help you until your condition deteriorates to the point where he has to drop everything and rush you in here."

She's trying to control her voice. "I don't ask him for anything unless I have to."

"For such a bright girl, that's not very smart. Listen,

he can't think about anything except you. Because you won't tell him honestly, he spends all day trying to guess how you're feeling, what you need, how he might help. He can't study any more—or probably do much of anything else. Haven't you noticed he's lost weight? That means he's not eating, and it's going to get worse until you do something about it."

She stares at me, hurt and furious, but I know I've made my point. I start to leave the room, turn back and speak more softly. "Rashi's devoting his life to your health, you know. I hope you'll take a few minutes to think about his."

And I'm out the door.

However, the Sitanis haunt me the rest of the morning, and at lunch break, a little after noon, I'm still thinking about them, about the woman injured by the drill press, and about Brian—the part fortune has played with them all, the options that are left to them. Fortune.

The food on my plate grows cold as I remember the cloudy morning I walked out the front door of my house in Philadelphia and started down the road, carrying a knapsack and a huge suitcase. I intended to hitchhike to New Mexico, to the university in Albuquerque—where I had been accepted for the special year of graduate study that could lead to my being accepted in medical school. Had someone said to me, "Look, we're going to tie your feet together, and if you want to get there, you're going to have to hop," I would have hopped.

Fat rainclouds were closing in overhead, but even so the day, to me, seemed blessed. I mean, how many times in your life do you start walking down the road toward your FUTURE?

Traveling day and night, I reached Albuquerque in four days.

When I checked in at the YMCA, the first thing I saw was a notice on a bulletin board announcing a meeting for premed students in the student union building at 11:00 that morning.

Now I don't know how I made this mistake, but somehow I got the idea that there were two meetings: one at 11:00 and another one immediately after. So I showered and changed and hitched a ride and got to the student union building at about noon—just as what I thought was the first meeting was letting out.

I sat down to wait for the second one to begin.

Well, it didn't take long for me to realize that I was, and would continue to be, the only one waiting; I had missed the meeting. Not even the sight of a cobra underneath my bed in Ethiopia aroused more panic in me than that moment. I had convinced myself I had no margin for error. With my lackluster academic background, I knew that if this year of special studies was indeed to open the doors into medical school I simply couldn't afford to make any wrong moves.

As I watched the man on the speaker's podium gather up his papers, I picked up the remnants of my self-esteem and went over to him. First, I told him how terrible I felt about missing the meeting; and then, how important it was for me to do well in my first year.

He wasn't an intimidating-looking man. He had hair graying at the temples, wore gold-rimmed glasses, was perhaps six inches shorter than I. He frowned a little bit, saying he didn't understand how I could have thought there were two meetings and that he was sorry, but that he had to go to lunch now.

Looking back, I can't believe I did this, but I asked him, "Well, could I eat lunch with you?"

I think I startled him so much, he didn't know what

to say. Finally he kind of half shrugged and said, "I suppose so."

We went to the cafeteria in the student union building. I didn't eat anything because I was too busy talking. I told that man about my Ethiopian experience, how determined I was to get into medical school, and that I would do anything in order to become a doctor—work as a missionary in the jungle, sleep out with the goats and pigs —whatever I had to do, I would. I asked him what courses I should take during this year of special studies, which professors it would be most beneficial for me to study with, etc. etc., until at last he'd had enough. He touched his napkin to his lips and stood up.

I stood too, and as he was edging around me to reach the aisle, I said, "Oh, by the way, I didn't catch your name." He didn't slow his pace at all—in fact, I think he increased it—but he said over his shoulder, "I'm Dr. Curran."

Good God. Dr. Curran. Dr. William Curran, dean of student affairs, the man who had corresponded with me in Ethiopia.

My legs stopped supporting me as I sank back into my chair, sprawling there, thinking what an ass I'd been. Within a two-hour span, not only had I missed an important meeting, I had alienated—probably forever—the one man whose encouragement was responsible for my coming to Albuquerque.

I went back to the Y, desperate to salvage some sort of hope. Finally I said to myself, "Sword, you're going to be a monk this year. You will sit in the front row of every class you take and you'll ask questions, dozens of them. The library will be your second home. You'll read extra books on every subject you are studying. In fact, you are going to become the ultimate—the epitome—of students. And at the end of this semester, you're going to visit Dean Curran just long enough to show him a set of A's, and tell him that in six months' time you'll be back to show him another set.

I did all of that.

The only time I wasn't in class or the library or studying, or sleeping, I was working (I'd gotten a job in one of the labs doing maintenance work).

I did get straight A's that semester; I did show Dean Curran, and when I brought him the second set of A's at the end of the second semester, he actually gave me a smile.

I was admitted into graduate school the following year with a major in biochemistry. The money I had earned serving with the Peace Corps had given out by then, but thanks to my good grades, I was hired as a teaching assistant.

I still wasn't positive I would be accepted into medical school the next year. The University of New Mexico has the smallest medical school in the United States. I knew 900 had applied, and only 36 would be accepted. But I felt the odds had definitely improved.

Then shortly after Thanksgiving, the letter came.

I was alone in the rooming house where I lived when I saw the envelope and realized what it was. With unsteady fingers I picked it up and opened it. The message inside was brief, just a couple of paragraphs, but I knew they held the answer to my future. When I understood that I had been accepted as a medical student, I started jumping up and down and yelling—and a moment later, there were tears mixed in with all that joy.

I had a girl friend by then, Kathleen (who, that summer, became my first wife), and I thought to myself, "Tell Kathleen! You've got to go over and tell her now." Not even stopping to telephone, I hurried to my car.

On the way to her apartment, I pulled up at a stop-

light across the street from a technical school where handicapped people went to learn a trade. I had stopped at
that light dozens of times before, watching those people
who were struggling to master skills most of us take for
granted.

This particular day the school was just letting out,
and as I sat in my car the students began to cross the street
in front of me. Some were quite young, obviously born
handicapped, while others, accident victims perhaps, were
older, trying to adjust to more recent afflictions. It seemed
to me then as if I were watching a parade in slow motion,
and something in me left whoever or what I was at that
moment (euphoric young man just accepted into medical
school) to walk with them across that street, so that I knew
something tinier than a pinpoint was all that separated me
from being that blind boy, that lame woman, the young
man with no hands. Suddenly I realized how quickly fortune can turn, and that each of us is at the mercy of the
unexpected. I also knew how well I must use everything
within myself, all that I was, to give back what life was
giving me.

12:35 P.M.—When I get back from lunch, the pace has
picked up. There are three charts bearing blue stickers in
the rack. Malone will be coming in at one o'clock to work
the relief shift until nine o'clock. If Sy or any of the other
emergency medicine physicians on the staff were due in, I
would be looking forward to the help. And once, I would
have looked forward to working with Malone.

When I joined the ER staff at Los Angeles Memorial,
he seemed to me to be a highly competent, caring ER
physician. We respected one another's abilities, and when
we were on the same shift we worked well together.

I did notice that he worked more night shifts than any other ER physician, and I asked Sy about that.

Sy said Malone had requested nights. The then-director of ER didn't like working nights. Given their choice, most of the other ER physicians on the staff preferred days too. So when Malone made his request, it was honored.

Sy said he didn't think it was a good idea, because it set Malone apart too much. He became, in fact, a kind of phantom. The only opportunity he had to interact with the other ER physicians was during the two-hour overlap in the evenings between seven and nine. And working nights also diminished his opportunity to interact with the physicians and technicians upstairs.

I knew, of course, from my own experience how many factors combine to make the emergency room a vulnerable place after dark, how alone you can feel. The patients who come in are usually sicker. Or more desperate, people who have nowhere else to go.

It's harder to get anything done because there are fewer people working in the hospital upstairs, fewer technicians in the lab, so you have to wait twice as long for test results. Only one operating room is kept open in the hospital; one surgery crew is available. And it would cost so much money to bring in another one, the hospital can rarely be persuaded to do it, no matter how bad things get.

If you're in doubt about an x-ray, there's no one to call to ask to come down and consult with you. And you think twice or even three times before phoning one of the on-call specialists at home at three o'clock in the morning to ask for an opinion.

I remember one Saturday night shift I had a few weeks after I came to L.A. Memorial, when I ended up playing musical chairs with the on-call staff. A fifty-five-year-old janitor had been shot in the chest a little after midnight. The bullet entered the neck at the sternal notch and came out at the scapula. The man was alert and talkative, although blood was bubbling from the hole in his neck, and there was considerable swelling around the wound. I immediately put an endotracheal tube down his nose and hooked him up to the breathing machine. His x-rays showed a hemopneumothorax on the right, and I inserted a chest tube in his right side. Fifteen hundred ccs of blood poured out of the chest tube, which we filtered and transfused back into him.

Then I called the general surgeon. The general surgeon said that it was a thoracic case and to call the thoracic surgeon.

The thoracic surgeon said it sounded like a head and neck case, but he agreed to come in and look at the man. After looking at him, he told me to transfer the patient to County. I wasn't especially surprised when County, after listening to a description of the man's wound, said he wasn't stable enough to transfer. The thoracic surgeon then said to call an ENT surgeon.

The ENT surgeon said it was beyond his ability unless a vascular surgeon ruled out any injury to the big vessels in the neck—the carotid, jugular, and esophagus.

The vascular surgeon I spoke to said he would take the case *if* a radiologist would first come in and do an angiogram.

A radiologist I called refused to come in unless the vascular surgeon were present when he did the angiogram.

I was fairly desperate by then, but fortunately the radiologist was a friend of mine, and I was able to persuade him to come in. He arrived at 4:00 A.M. The angiogram was negative, meaning no major vessels were damaged in the neck. The bullet had ruptured the trachea and the lungs.

When I relayed this information to the vascular surgeon he said it was out of his ballpark since no major vessels were involved, and to call the ENT surgeon.

The ENT surgeon agreed to take the case and perform surgery in the morning. So, at 6:30 A.M., the patient was admitted to the hospital. I had managed the case, alone, for over six hours.

After that experience, I couldn't imagine why anyone would actually choose the night shift over the day shift.

"It started when his second marriage was breaking up," Sy explained. "And his wife worked days. So it got him out of the house when she was most apt to be home. After their divorce, he kept on doing it because I think working nights gave him a sense of control. You're definitely the one in charge around here at night. You make all the decisions. And if everything else in your life is disintegrating, maybe you look forward to this one time and place that you can control. But I don't think it's a good idea, not for him, not for anyone."

I didn't think it was a good idea either. And when the ER director resigned to move to San Diego, and I applied for and was given the position, I took steps to change things. I rearranged the shift schedule so that Malone didn't work any more nights than the rest of us.

He didn't like that.

And later, when I observed how distressed he was by the downward spiral his third marriage was taking, and gave him as many of the 1:00 to 9:00 swing shifts as possible so that he wouldn't be alone on duty, he liked that even less.

For the past several weeks, his behavior has been disturbingly erratic. He alternates between being hyper-cheerful and being sunk in a bog of depression. He's either coming on with the nurses and any attractive female patients he happens to treat; or he's slogging from room to room as though he's trying to get through a swamp, not looking anyone in the eye, and leaving the patients, Illana says, in worse psychological shape than they were before he saw them. Sometimes he will move from one extreme to the other within the span of his shift.

Staff physicians and nurses in other departments are beginning to talk about him, and I know I can't allow the situation to continue. The last thing an ER director wants to do is have the hospital administration focus negative attention on the emergency room. The administration is sharply aware that the emergency room is often the interface between the hospital and the public, that many patients who enter the hospital for the first time do so through the emergency room. And of course they want us to give as positive an impression as possible.

Also, because ER physicians work on a thirty-day contract with the hospital, there is a certain aura of expendability that hovers over us. If one among us isn't working up to par, we tend to feel we're all in jeopardy.

Those are the hard facts of life I have to weigh in this situation with Michael Malone. I suspect before this month is out I'm going to have to let him go.

But right now I have no time to worry about Malone. I take the top chart out of the rack, scanning it as I walk down the corridor toward the ENT room. The patient is Jane Byrd, a thirty-six-year-old professor at a large nearby university. She has been stabbed in the neck.

When I enter the room, she is lying still on the bed, her eyes open. She has long, straight black hair, pale skin, gray-blue eyes. If Sy were here, I might tell him she looks like a Celtic poetess and watch him roll his eyes toward the ceiling.

The stab wound on the left side of Jane Byrd's neck is small but deep, oozing bright red blood. There is a fair amount of swelling, more than there should be if it were just venous blood. The wound is in a vulnerable place, where several vital organs are in close proximity: the trachea, the esophagus, carotid arteries.

As we begin to talk, I ask her what subject she teaches, and she replies, medieval English literature. She tells me in a distant, almost abstracted way what happened to her. This phenomenon of depersonalizing an event by intellectualizing it is something I've seen before.

An extreme instance I witnessed was during my rotating internship in my first postgraduate year. I was doing a six-week stint in ob/gyn when a woman delivered a Down's syndrome baby. The obstetrician said nothing to the mother during delivery, but after she had been taken to the recovery room he explained to me he preferred to tell the husband and wife together when such things happened. Then he asked if I wanted to be present when he told them.

I knew if I needed exposure to anything at that point in my career, it was how to deal with raw human emotion. They don't teach you about that in medical school. The first year you study the normal body; the second year you study the diseased body; at no point do you study the emotional body.

I said to the obstetrician, yes, I would like to be present.

The parents were sensitive, intelligent people in their late thirties who had only been married a couple of years. They already suspected something was wrong because their baby hadn't been brought to them, and the two other mothers in the recovery room were, at that moment, holding their newborns, sharing these moments with their husbands.

The obstetrician pulled the screening curtain around the bed, then quietly told the couple their newborn son had Down's syndrome and would be profoundly retarded.

For several moments, neither of them spoke.

Finally, the husband cleared his throat and asked—in the same tone he might have used to inquire about the stock market—what the statistics were on such a thing happening to people in their age group.

The obstetrician was obviously relieved to be able to talk about numbers. After he had answered the husband's questions, the wife inquired what the IQ range was among mongoloid children.

So there was this statistical discussion going on, and yet I could feel the subterranean tide of emotion in that room, searching for some kind of opening. The man's and woman's eyes had the brightness only certain kinds of agony impart, even as they remained rational and civilized.

At Los Angeles Memorial, that kind of distancing of oneself from emotion doesn't happen often.

Recently I had to tell a Latin woman her husband had been shot to death, and moments later she locked herself in the shower room where we'd placed his sheeted body. She wailed for almost an hour in a voice loud enough to carry the full length of the corridor and into the ambulance parking area as well. As I listened to her, I thought how much healthier it was to meet the situation instantly and to start letting out the agony.

People helping others cope with tragedy often come to me and ask me to administer a shot, a tranquilizer, to someone who has just lost a husband or wife or child. I explain to them that giving a shot only postpones grief, it doesn't make it go away, and grieving is something that must eventually be gotten through. However, I tell them if the bereaved person wants a shot and comes, personally, to ask me, I will administer one. But rarely do they come. Occasionally they will ask me for a prescription to take home—yet I suspect they use it as something they can hold in reserve, like a security blanket.

Emotion, whether it be grief or anger, needs expression.

I know someday Jane Byrd will have to let hers out too, but right now she speaks so softly I have to bend my head down to hear.

"Tell me how this happened," I say.

"I was alone in my office," she answers, "grading papers. There was a noon rally of some kind in the quad, and the building was practically empty. When I heard footsteps in the hallway come to a stop outside my office, I looked up. There's an opaque glass panel in the door, and I could see somebody's shadow there. So I was—I was staring at the door when it opened and this—this man came in. He shut the door softly behind him, I remember that."

She hesitated.

"Go on," I said.

"Well, he was a tall man—unshaven; long, dark-blond hair. He wore a gold earring with a red stone in it.

"He told me to go ahead and scream if I wanted to, because nobody would hear, and he liked listening to women scream. And then he said women who chose to be alone in places deserved whatever happened to them.

"He moved toward me while he was talking, and I didn't say anything at all. I could feel my heart beating very fast, and yet it was almost like I was watching this on television.

"And then he was standing next to me, pulling my hair back with one hand so hard it hurt, and with the other hand he was holding a knife against my neck, and he was saying, 'Give me your money.'

"I guess that was the point it began to seem real. I—I'm vain about my hair. Right then I didn't care anything about him taking my money, I just wanted him to stop touching my hair.

"I keep my purse in the bottom left-hand drawer of my desk, so when I reached down to open it, he must not have understood what I was doing, because he—he jerked my head back harder, and I felt the knife being pressed more deeply into my neck.

"Then we both heard the sound of a door opening and shutting in the hallway. He—he suddenly stuck the knife into my neck, then pulled it out, and ran.

"I picked up the phone and called security and they were there in minutes. They wanted to call the paramedics, but the wound seemed so small to me, I told them I would drive myself to the hospital. And I did."

She gives me a small, almost apologetic smile, and I am struck simultaneously by two things: how completely she has succeeded, for the moment, in shutting the emotional part of herself away from the fact that she has been violently assaulted and wounded. The second thing is— how goddam wonderful it is to have an articulate patient.

I concentrate on her wound. I've never liked ENT. I can't see where things are well enough. I'm not absolutely certain now, but I think I can detect bubbles of subcutaneous air beneath her skin. Feeling these tiny bubbles is an eerie sensation. It feels and sounds as if you're touching Rice Krispies. If you press down lightly, your fingertips displace the air bubbles, leaving a mark almost like a fingerprint on the skin. The presence of air beneath Jane

Byrd's skin could mean the tip of the knife blade penetrated her trachea. If that's true she needs immediate
surgery.

I phone ENT upstairs. The on-call specialist is in the
operating room on a complicated case that could last for
hours, so I ask for the backup, and after several minutes he
comes on the line. Unfortunately, he's eighty miles away in
Palm Springs, but he listens to my description of the
wound and suggests I call upstairs for a vascular surgeon. I
do. The surgeon I speak to says to keep the woman under
observation for a couple of hours and to let him know if
anything changes.

I'm not satisfied with that, so while I'm trying to
figure out what to do next, wishing Sy were on duty since
he's doing a residency in this area, the ENT specialist who
had been in OR when I first called comes down to look at
Jane Byrd. After examining her, he says he wants to do
exploratory surgery at once.

"G-g-g-g-g-good," I hear myself saying. He gives me a
brief surprised look, and I leave the room quickly while he
fills out the papers to have her transferred upstairs.

I don't stutter much any more. But when I was a kid,
the problem was severe. I don't remember when my
tongue started tying itself into knots, but my mother tells
me it was some time in the second grade, and I haven't a
clue as to why. Stuttering is one of life's mysteries. There
are a lot of intelligent theories about cause and treatment.
However, the most that can be said of them is that some of
them work for some people some of the time. None of
them worked for me.

My memories of my acute stuttering are vivid: when I
couldn't get a word out, I would clench my fists so hard my
fingernails would cut into my palms. If the teacher happened to call on me in class, and I knew the answer but

my stuttering prevented my tongue from getting it out, I would bite my lip until it bled; sometimes I even hit myself to try and make the words come out. If anyone in class teased me, I'd fly at him like a maniac.

When I was in the middle of third grade, we moved five miles, from Glenolden to Springfield, which meant I had to enter a new school. For weeks before the move I litanized, "You will not stutter in the new school . . . you will not stutter . . . you will not." Of course I stuttered the very first time I was asked to speak and I still do when I'm upset or extremely insecure.

So even though I sometimes find myself yearning for articulate patients like Jane Byrd, I certainly remember what it was like to be inarticulate and powerless. And when I see others on my staff grow impatient with people who can't verbalize the symptoms of their illnesses, or when I feel my own temper thinned to the snapping point, I tell myself, "You remember, Sword, what it's like," and I try harder then to let my fingers, my eyes, do the detective work.

1:07 P.M.—Malone is here. He is a small, wiry man with a bristle of red hair, hazel eyes flecked with so many other colors they change depending on his mood, what color shirt he's wearing, or the light he's standing in. He walks with a taut, springy step as though his calf muscles were made of elastic. As he passes by me now in the corridor carrying a patient's chart, he does a fast soft-shoe and flashes me a brilliant smile. I can see right away it's one of his manic days.

Illana, whose professionalism could set the standard for nursing, is fed up with Malone's mood swings. Alfred is deeply concerned. Eugene is fascinated. "It's like working with identical twins," I heard him say to Alfred, "and you never know which one's on." I think it's reaching the point where if I don't do something, I'm going to lose Illana.

But so far, despite his mood swings, Malone has continued to perform well on the job, although I have noticed brief lapses in his judgment. Last week one of the nurses told me Malone issued orders to give an enema to a pregnant girl with abdominal pains without first determining that she wasn't in early labor. Then he rescinded them five minutes later.

Having just gone through my own divorce, I empathize with the man's plight—so much so that I've begun discussing Malone's problems during my appointments with my therapist, Allen. In fact lately Allen is apt to say, "Well, who's the star of the session today, you or Malone?" Yet whenever we do talk about Malone, the discussions seem to be particularly meaningful for me. When I mentioned this to Allen, he just gave me one of his cryptic smiles.

Allen does, fortunately, know a lot about burnout. "It's an interesting syndrome," he told me. "As far as I know, it never affects underachievers or moderates. Its victims are often like Malone: charismatic, impatient individuals who expect too much from life. They either can't or won't accept any limitations or restrictions, and they expect the energy they invest to provide rewards equal to their efforts. But that doesn't happen—especially in the helping professions. This is why teachers, doctors, nurses, police, and social workers are so often disillusioned.

"Sometimes, of course, they're impeded by the system —bureaucracy, administrators; but more often, they're stopped by the fact that the goals they've set for themselves are simply unreachable."

"You know, I can imagine the hopes Malone had when he entered medicine. Yet the patient population that he sees is, for the most part, totally indifferent to how good a doctor he might be. The marriages he hoped would shore up his ego have turned out, apparently, to be exercises in despair. And from what you tell me he's driven almost all his friends away.

"Unless he finds another attitude, a new way to deal with that terrible need he has to be the best, to change the world, I don't see much hope for him."

Grim prognosis.

To date, I haven't seen Malone's downward spiral interfering with his ability to care for the physical needs of his patients. Yet I sense the potential of that happening. When I do a hypothetical chart review with him and we discuss the treatment that could or should be rendered a fictional patient (something I do periodically with every doctor on my staff), Malone's responses are always clinically on target, often brilliantly inductive; and yet there is something that makes me uneasy. It's almost as though the intellectual process of finding the answer has become more important to him than helping the patient.

But it's an intangible, nothing I can quantify or define clearly enough even to be able to talk about with Sy. Still, I *am* worried, so much so that I've tried to arrange Malone's and my schedules so that his shifts overlap with mine. That way I can watch him.

I should be watching him right now, especially since he's manic and therefore vulnerable to a sudden mood swing in the opposite direction. But when I glance at the chart rack, there is a virtual sea of blue stickers.

In quick succession I see . . .

—Per Stolleson, a retired sea captain from Copenhagen who set up housekeeping with an East Indian woman six weeks ago, and after eating her spicy-hot curries for that length of time swelled up like a dirigible, his whole Nordic system in a state of outrage. "Voorth it, though," he tells me with a slow wink, "voorth every gott dom minute of it."

—Alfonse Gerraldo, a worker in the stockyards, who came in with a bullet wound in the palm of his right hand. Alfonse doesn't speak English, so I ask Ramon, our Spanish-speaking orderly, to translate for me. Ramon is an excellent interpreter, skilled at getting panicky patients to relax, then eliciting information from them and passing it along to me as quickly as he can.

Yet speaking in Spanish strikes me as taking longer; it seems somehow slower, more circuitous. For example, if I say to Ramon, "Ask him where it hurts," which is a five-syllable sentence, it seems to take Ramon as many as thirty syllables to phrase this question, and the patient another thirty to answer it.

I mentioned this once to Sy, and he said, "True, Spanish isn't as concise or clinical as English, but time warp is involved, too, and when you know seconds are vital, their passing seems interminable."

Then he added, "You, Sword, you're going to feel like that whether a patient is critical or not. It's part of your itchy-finger syndrome."

Since he said that to me, I've tried—without much success—to curb my impatience when I have to get answers through a translator. I am fairly patient now as I examine Alfonse's wound, which is painful and entails a long healing process, but isn't serious.

"Ask him how it happened," I tell Ramon.

Alfonse, refusing to look at either of us, responds to Ramon's questions in soft monosyllables.

"He was told to shoot a pig," Ramon tells me. "The

pig squealed when he started toward it, and he doesn't know how it happened, but he grew careless, didn't look where he was stepping, and slipped in some pig shit. As he fell, he shot himself in the hand."

Alfonse's eyes seem to be glued to the floor.

"Listen," I say to Ramon, "tell him about the cop who came in two nights ago, the one who shot himself in the foot playing quickdraw."

Ramon does.

Alfonse looks up slowly. "He—shoot foot?"

"*Sí.*"

"Policeman?"

Ramon nods.

"Ah." Alfonse smiles.

He and Ramon are still discussing the incident when I leave the room to see . . .

—Jane Doe, a "jumper," a woman in her late twenties who jumped out a second-story window. She has a tattoo on her left breast, a red heart with a jagged line cleaving it in half, and three green tears emerging from the place where the heart is broken. Her breath smells of alcohol; she's unconscious, although she moans softly when I rub her sternum. I check her pupils, examine her skull, look for malocclusion and fracture of the upper jaw; palpate her pharynx, neck, abdomen; check her reflexes. I don't find anything, but I know from past experience jumpers are prone to the gravest kind of internal injuries, so I order blood drawn, a urinalysis, x-rays of her neck, back, skull, chest, and pelvis, and then I go to see . . .

—Artie Hayes and Harry Mills, two morticians who have come in for shots of gamma globulin because the last cadaver they worked on died of hepatitis.

Scanning the charts, I note one of them, Artie, has alarmingly high blood pressure, 220/120.

"Which one of you is Artie?" I ask.

They look at each other, grin, and for a beat, they don't say anything. Then they point at each other and say simultaneously, "He's Artie," and I get the feeling these two have been together for a long, long time.

One of them is tall and thin, with a small, neatly clipped moustache. The other one is rotund, wearing a dazzling chartreuse tie. I suppose I would pick the one with the tie to be Artie because of the excess weight, although that's certainly not an infallible indicator.

"He does the bodies," the one with the moustache says.

"And he does the faces," the other rejoins.

The moustache: "So who's most likely to get hepatitis?"

The necktie: "The face man, or the body man?"

I ask, "Do either of you have an open cut that came in contact with the cadaver when you were working on it?"

They look at each other.

"I don't," the moustache says. "But you nicked yourself when you were shaving that morning, didn't you, Artie?"

"Yeah, but my chin didn't come anywhere near Mr. Pilbean," the short one replies. "I didn't kiss him or anything."

At least I know now which one is Artie.

"Then your chances of getting hepatitis are one in ten thousand," I say. "You probably don't even need the shot, but I'll give it to you just to be on the safe side."

"Do Artie first," Harry tells me, "so I can watch him pass out."

"Naw, start with Harry," Artie says. "I love it when he cries."

"Listen, Artie," I say, "your blood pressure is pretty high. How long since you've had a physical checkup?"

He grows serious for the first time. "Well, I—I don't know."

"How high is it?" Harry wants to know.

"Too high. He needs to see a doctor, have some blood tests, a urinalysis, get some medication to bring it down."

"You're a doctor," Artie says. "Can't you prescribe something?"

"He means a regular doctor," Harry says.

And Artie asks, "Aren't you a regular doctor?"

"I am," I say wryly, "but ER doctors usually don't prescribe for chronic conditions or become involved in long-term care of patients. Our function is to be immediately available to acutely ill or injured patients. It would be advisable for you to get continuing care from your family doctor, someone who knows you."

When I see worry beginning to form in Harry's eyes, I say to him, "Will you see that he goes to someone? And I don't mean next month."

"You bet. As soon as we get out of here."

I write the orders on the chart for the gamma globulin, and as I leave the room I hear Harry say, "Damn it, Artie, how many times have I told you to go on a diet!"

"Listen," Artie replies, "if I kick off, I want you to do my face in Number Four Rose Blush. Or . . . or maybe I'd look better in Sunset Glow. What do you think?"

"Artie—"

"Huh?"

"Can it."

2:37 P.M.—I step out into the corridor and almost collide with Alfred. A half hour ago he was relieved at the triage desk, and he looks exhausted. "Paramedics just brought in a scoop and run," he tells me. "Gunshot wound in the jaw."

When the police or paramedics find a victim so close to a hospital that it would take less time to bring him or her to the emergency room than it would to provide any treatment on the scene, they bring the patient directly to ER. This is called a scoop and run. If they're fairly close to several hospitals, they will contact the base station for instructions about which hospital can best accommodate the patient.

"Where's Malone?" I ask.

"In the main treatment room with a new admit, Mrs. Murphy . . . cardiac arrhythmia. We've called Dr. Ahmad, but you know what that means. As long as the patient isn't in full cardiac arrest, it could be hours before he gets down here. She's hooked up to the monitor now; Dr. Malone's initiated a lidocaine drip, and I'm going to help him monitor her."

Unlike Illana, Alfred has never confronted me about Malone. Nor will he. But he is sharply aware whenever ER is not running as smoothly as it should. And if he sees a way that he can help correct the balance, he will do so.

His telling me now what he's going to be doing is a way of letting me know he'll be near Malone while I'm busy with the trauma victim. It isn't the first time I've been the recipient of his solicitude. There have been days (and nights) when I've wondered if I really can go on spending most of my life in the white corridor. Alfred, seeming to sense this, will work alongside me at such times, talking softly about things far removed from the emergency room—the new play at the Shubert, the tulips blooming in Leucadia, a musician he heard in the park. It helps.

I give him an appreciative nod and go on into the trauma room. Illana is taking the pulse of a middle-aged Latino lying on the Stryker bed closest to the far wall. Dennis stands nearby, watching. The man is conscious, moaning softly behind clenched lips. His eyes, frenzied with pain, keep darting from corner to corner of the ceiling. I see where the bullet entered on the right side of his jaw, and I wonder where it has lodged. Depending on the path it took, it could be impinging on the spinal cord.

I order x-rays stat, IVs, and CBC, and ask Illana, "Does he understand English?"

"Yes."

I bend over the man, saying, "Don't move your head. It's important that you keep still."

The frenzied eyes focus long enough on mine so that I know he has understood.

The x-ray technician wheels her machine into the room, beginning to position it alongside the patient. While she is arranging her plate where she wants it, Dennis enquires softly if he can watch, and the technician hands him a lead apron to put on.

Illana and I step out into the corridor and Illana says, "The man's son is in the waiting room, talking to Ramon. He's only about six or seven years old. I guess he saw it happen."

The x-ray machine whines loudly and clicks twice.

I think of my daughter, Alexis, who will be six on her next birthday. At this time of day Alexis is getting home from kindergarten. The school she attends has a separate "pod" for the kindergarten class. It's a small Roman–brick building with windows opening onto an enclosed play area sheltered by shade trees. There are tricycles, wagons, a bin where building blocks are kept. While this man's son watched his father get shot in the face, Alexis was probably riding a tricycle around the play area or sitting with the other children listening to her teacher read a story.

"Counterproductive," Sy would tell me if he knew what I was thinking. "Fortune is blind, Sword. Don't try to give it eyes. Help when you can. That's all you can do."

Two policemen enter the corridor through the ambulance entrance and ask me where the gunshot victim is. I nod toward the trauma room, but tell them, "He's been shot in the jaw. He can't talk."

The younger one says, "Yeah, well, we need to get a description of the assailant."

"Not now!" I snap.

There is a long beat of silence. Finally I murmur, "Sorry."

Illana suggests softly, "Maybe the boy could tell them something that would help." Because she lives with a policeman, Illana tries harder than anyone else to be helpful to them.

The x-ray technician comes out of the trauma room, and in answer to the silent question in my eyes murmurs, "Five minutes."

I say to the policemen, "Okay if I talk to the boy for a few minutes first?"

The older cop says, "Sure, go ahead."

I'm still haunted by the difference between the boy's life and Alexis's. I have a mental picture of this kid who has watched his father get shot in the face being confronted by two policemen in dark uniforms, gleaming holsters, and nightsticks, and I think somebody should tell him first what it is they want.

Illana goes back into the trauma room and I walk to the opposite end of the corridor, press the button that opens the doors, and enter the waiting room.

Ramon is sitting beside the boy on a couch in the corner. The television set on the wall opposite them is turned to a rerun of *The Partridge Family*. The boy's face is streaked with dirt and tears. He holds an open can of Sprite, but he isn't drinking it. Near his feet are two Alpha Beta shopping bags, and as I draw near I see oranges inside.

I pull up a chair and sit down beside Ramon. "Is he okay?"

Ramon answers, "He's scared to death."

"The police want to talk to him. Has he been able to tell you what happened?"

"Yeah. He says he and his father went to Santa Ana last night. The owner of an orchard there told them they could have the oranges that had fallen on the ground. And this morning they began selling the oranges on the street. They were standing near the corner of Washington and Figueroa when a man pulls over to the curb and asks to try one. The boy's father tells him it will cost him ten cents to try one, and the man pulls out a gun and shoots him."

I look at the boy. His eyes are on the TV screen.

"Ask him if he thinks he could describe this man to the police."

Ramon puts the question to the boy, and I hear the answer, *"Si."*

Then the boy says something more to Ramon in Spanish.

Ramon translates. "He wants to know if his father is going to be all right."

I could say "Yes," just to make him feel better. But I don't. "I don't know," I say. "Tell him I will let him know as soon as I see the x-rays."

While Ramon is translating this, I walk away, punch

the numbers on the code buttons that unlock the doors—5-5-5-5 (thinking, as I often have before, how easy it would be for anybody watching who wanted to memorize that code to do so).

I tell the waiting policemen the boy can probably help them, then look in the x-ray box. The developed negatives are there.

I go back into the trauma room and clip them to the light board. The right side of the man's jaw looks like shattered crystal. I count the pieces—one, two, three, four, five. The bullet has lodged in the back of the neck in a safe zone—that is, it's not impinging on the spinal cord or any vital organ lateral to the midline.

It will be a long time before he is well again. But he will eventually be all right, and I send Dennis to tell his son.

3:14 P.M.—I walk down the corridor, glancing into the treatment rooms, looking for Malone.

I'm sure he's begun to sense I'm watching him. I thought I might be able to get away with it, because, as Sy tells me, "Sword, you're a damn busybody." Once when Sy was treating a gunshot wound to the abdomen I hovered beside him, asking if he'd gotten x-rays, if he'd put in a catheter, started a second IV, done this, done that. Finally he looked me straight in the eye and said, "Would you rather I went out to a movie?"

It's a problem I have. When I'm confronted with a life-threatening situation, I feel like I *have* to participate—no matter how competent the doctor in charge is.

The other EM physicians on staff here have grown fairly tolerant of my constant need to oversee the critical cases, and I'd hoped Malone would accept my close scrutiny of him as part of my itchy-finger syndrome. He may have, for a while. Not any more.

Alfred enters the corridor from the main treatment room, and I ask him where Malone is.

"Ob/gyn," he says. I can tell from the tone of his voice something is wrong.

"What is it, Alfred?"

He hesitates, and I am at once aware of the quandary he is in. Alfred hasn't minded watching over Malone. But I should have anticipated the moment when he would have to do more than that.

"He's—well, he has two difficult cases," Alfred says softly. "Dr. Ahmad still hasn't come down, and Mrs. Murphy's arrhythmia isn't responding to medication. And he has a young girl in ob/gyn complaining of abdominal pain who won't submit to a pelvic examination."

Nothing Alfred's said has implied any criticism of Malone. But we both know that for him to explicate Malone's cases at all implies there is trouble.

I cross the corridor quickly and enter ob/gyn.

Malone and Illana are standing on one side of the treatment bed where a frail-looking girl with light-brown hair and intense, almost electric-blue eyes is sitting up in a hunched, defensive position. She doesn't look older than twelve. A thin, tired-looking woman whose eyes may once have been the same blue is standing on the other side of the bed.

Illana looks tense, angry, though she's trying not to let the anger show, and I'm not sure who it's directed at.

Malone's face is full of rage.

The girl, clearly in pain, is holding tightly to the hem of her hospital gown with both hands. "Mama, don't let him touch me there."

"She's going to have to have a pelvic exam, or I can't help her," Malone says tightly.

"She's been taught to keep herself private," the mother says. "I don't see why you have to look at her there."

"Because if she's pregnant," Malone replies, "we all need to know it."

The woman's eyes widen. "Hattie isn't pregnant! Why, she's barely even . . . barely even . . ." She doesn't finish.

The girl flashes Malone a venomous look out of those electric eyes, then whimpers, "Mama, I don't like it here. I want to go home."

Malone has painted himself into a corner.

There is a rule in ER: any female with abdominal distress—no matter how young or old—is pregnant until proven otherwise. And every suspected pregnancy is an ectopic pregnancy until proven otherwise. In other words, suspect the worst and then prove yourself wrong.

If the patient denies she is pregnant, you have to find some way to examine her without arousing her suspicion that you believe she may be pregnant.

If a parent or relative is present, that can complicate the situation because often a female will confide things to you when she is alone that she simply cannot tell you in the presence of a family member.

On the other hand, if a young girl is truly ill and the parent is worried, you can often appeal to the parent and elicit some support. The worst thing you can do is imply you think the patient is lying.

Malone turns to me, his voice is still angry as he says, "Is there something you wanted, doctor?"

"I thought maybe I could lend a hand."

"One doctor and one nurse is usually sufficient."

I ignore that and ask, "May I see the chart?"

Illana holds it out to me.

The girl's name is Hattie Spencer. She is thirteen. She complained of upper abdominal pain this morning; also nausea and dry heaves. The pain was crampy at first and then became constant, and within the past hour has migrated to her lower abdomen. She has painful and frequent urination.

The notes further state the patient claims to have had no sexual activity of any kind. She started menstruating at the age of eleven, but her periods have always been irregular so she doesn't know whether her period is late this month or not.

Her vital signs are good; her blood pressure is a little low, perhaps. Her heart rate is 112, which is a little high; her white count is 15,000, indicating possible infection or stress somewhere. Her hematocrit is 30—too low.

"Did you get a urine sample?" I ask. That's usually the easiest way to confirm a suspected pregnancy.

"It was contaminated with stool," Malone replies sharply. "Now she says she can't 'go' any more. She also says it's impossible for her to be pregnant."

Talking about her as "she" in her presence draws another hostile glance from the girl.

"You'd better do a cath urine, then," I say.

"I was just about to," he responds. "Any other instructions, doctor?"

He wants me out of there. I am loath to leave but have no reason to stay. He's doing everything by the book.

"It might help if you lighten up," I say.

"Oh, right," he says, and clicks his heels together.

I think I'd better leave before I make matters worse by really losing my temper with Malone. There's already enough anger in that room. I go back out into the corridor. What the hell am I going to do about him?

My concern and my discussions with Allen have led me to do some reading on my own on the subject of burnout.

It's a chronic condition, apparently; something a person moves toward over a period of months, even years. And just like any other chronic disease, there are several stages, each one a little bit worse than the last.

A lot of people experience short-term burnout after cramming for an exam, coping with a family illness, or pressuring themselves to get a project finished. To handle the aftermath of such episodes, they simply stop and take a rest.

But people like Malone don't allow themselves to rest. So catalyzing the burnout process is a bone-deep exhaustion that is hard for the person burning out to accept, because it's such a complete reversal from the high energy level he or she is used to. "Tomorrow," they tell themselves, "I'll be my old self again." Only they aren't.

Eventually their exhaustion causes impatience with themselves. Then with others, until finally they turn on those closest to them, blaming family members and co-workers for the mistakes they themselves are making because they're tired all the time.

And that, in turn, causes a kind of alienation. Every time people burning out feel disappointed or betrayed—and in their overly vulnerable state they feel that way a lot—they begin to say defensively, "What the hell, I don't care any more anyway," thereby distancing themselves from the involvements that offer their only hope for salvation.

Malone has done so much of that, the only friend he has left on the staff is Sy, and I don't know how much longer Sy is going to put up with him.

But how do you halt the burnout process? When I put that question to Allen, he told me, "Randy, you're asking me to judge the psychological state of a man I've never met. I can't do that. And I can't tell *you* what to do. If you want to, give him my name. Tell him I'd be happy to talk with him. Although if your description of the man's behavior is accurate, he probably can't accept the fact that he needs help. I can tell you you're wise to be watchful. The final stage of burnout is one of disorientation, when the concentration span is shot. And that, of course, could be disastrous where patient care is involved."

So I am watchful—along with Sy and everybody else who works with the man. Is it fair to put that much added stress on my staff? Shouldn't I just confront Malone? Yet every time I am about to do that, I am stopped by the hunted look in his eyes.

Malone may not know he's burning out. But he does know his third marriage is about over. He knows he's overextended financially with child support and alimony for his first two wives, while he's trying to maintain the lifestyle he promised his third one.

And he also knows that every day (or night) he comes to work, he sees people who are worse off than he is.

4:23 P.M.—Calvin tells me Sandra's on the phone. She probably just wants to ask me what time I'm going to pick up the girls on Saturday. These days we talk to each other like computer programmers, exchanging bits of non-threatening information.

I go into the doctors' room to take the call, telling her I'll come for the girls at ten, and she says good-bye and hangs up. The white-hot anger we felt toward each other right after the divorce is cooling. Two months ago she wouldn't have bothered to say good-bye.

I replace the receiver, but don't get up. It feels so good to be sitting down. You keep moving along that corridor, and you somehow forget or at least postpone knowing how tired you are.

I have just given myself permission to stay there for two more minutes when Malone enters. He's not happy to see me.

"I didn't think you ever took a break, Sword. Isn't that how you got to be director?"

I don't respond to the barb, asking him instead, "So did you get a cath urine on that girl?"

He shakes his head. "She left."

"She what?!"

"She left. The mother said she'd take her to see a doctor whose office is near where they live. Don't worry, I got her to sign an AMA [against medical advice]."

"I'm not worried about the AMA," I retort. "I'm worried about the girl. She was ill, Michael."

"I know that, but she wouldn't let me near her. You should have heard the names she called me when I tried to catheterize her. Worse than any street kid I ever treated."

"Did you talk to the mother alone, try to get her support?"

"Why the third degree, Sword? Don't tell me you've never had a patient AMA on you."

"Not one that sick," I want to say. But it isn't true. We've all had patients leave the hospital against medical advice who should have stayed. Sometimes they leave because they're scared, sometimes because they're angry or because they feel they've been put down by a staff member (usually Eugene). Each time it happens to me, I feel I've failed somehow. And I believe this situation could have been saved. I think the mother was reachable.

"Did the mother understand how sick the girl was?" I persist.

"I told her it could be serious, yes! I told her we needed to do some more tests. The girl started whining, and the mother gave in and they left. Now will you get off my back!"

I am silent, thinking about the girl. I am hoping fervently that Malone did make it clear to the mother that her daughter could be and probably was seriously ill. I know my doubt and anxiety show in my face. I also know Malone needs a few minutes alone.

"Take a break," I say. "I'll keep the lid on things for a while." And I get up out of my chair, heading for the corridor.

But suddenly he sidesteps his way in front of me. "The hell you will! I'm one of the best damn doctors on this staff, Sword, and you know it. So there is one favor I'd like to ask, if it isn't too much trouble."

"What's that?"

"Stop overlapping your shifts with mine. I was working in this emergency room before you ever got here, and I don't need you pulling guard duty just to watch me!" He hurries out into the corridor, goes to the chart rack, takes out the top chart, scans it, and strides into the main treatment room.

Worry about Hattie Spencer gnaws at me so much, I know it isn't going to go away until I've spoken to the mother. I ask Calvin to retrieve the chart and get Mrs. Spencer on the phone. But when he tries, there is no answer. I tell him to keep trying.

During the next hour and a half, Malone is a dynamo.

Around five-thirty, we get the usual influx of sick children brought in by parents who have been working during the day. When we listen to too much squalling, we begin to feel like we're carrying some of them around inside our heads, so if there are two doctors on duty and the flow of patients allows it, we try to alternate seeing the sick kids.

Not this afternoon. Malone takes every one that comes in and manages to treat other patients as well. If I wanted to keep up with him, I'd need roller skates. Twice when he passes me in the corridor, he gives me a smile with an edge on it and says, "Take a few minutes, Sword. I'll keep the lid on things."

At one point when we're both checking on patients in the main treatment room (I'm looking in on Jane Doe and Malone's with Mrs. Murphy), I hear him tell Alfred to switch the lidocaine drip to bretylium, and to call Ahmad again and tell him to get down here.

We've had trouble before when Dr. Ahmad has been the on-call cardiologist. He's an exchange doctor from Lebanon. The man is a good physician, but he has a penchant for taking incredibly long case histories from patients. Part of the reason for it, Alfred tells me, is Ahmad's difficulty with English; he's also terribly afraid of making a mistake in this country, and so he probes and probes. If he happens to be taking a history from a cardiac patient who is occupying a bed in our trauma room, I get extremely nervous—because I know access to the beds and crash carts can be needed by new patients at a moment's notice.

And if he's upstairs when I need him in ER, I'm also nervous, because I know he may be involved in taking one of his tortuous histories while *my* patient—who needs to be admitted into an intensive care unit upstairs—languishes.

I linger behind the closed curtain around Jane Doe's bed realizing how much I am beginning to resent this eggshell-walking I am doing on Malone's behalf. When he leaves, I step out from the curtain and pause by Mrs. Murphy's bed while Alfred is making the change in the IV that Malone requested. A glance up at the screen of the cardiac monitor tells me she's experiencing PVCs or premature ventricular contractions, one of the more common arrhythmias.

All normal electrical activity of the heart starts from a small bundle of muscle fibers and nerves, called the sinatrial node or pacemaker. The activity travels in a wave spread along well-defined pathways, causing the muscles of the heart to contract in a rhythmic fashion. It's a little like a rock thrown into a quiet pond that causes waves to spread and touch all the shores at a set interval of rhythm.

With PVCs like Mrs. Murphy's, it's as though another rock had been thrown into the pond from the other side, causing the wave pattern to be disrupted. The fact that her PVCs haven't responded to the lidocaine is unusual. But Malone's choice of bretylium as an alternate is a good one.

I can tell from the worried look in Alfred's eyes that he's concerned about Mrs. Murphy. Her blood pressure is slowly falling; if she goes into cardiogenic shock, a Swan-Ganz catheter will have to be put in. I make a mental note to tell Andy Donahue to keep an eye on her when he comes in to relieve me at seven.

I certainly don't like having to tell Andy to police one of Malone's patients. It puts him in an awkward position. And I am more aware than ever that my hope of keeping this situation contained until I find a way to help Malone just isn't going to work.

Things finally taper off around six o'clock—which isn't unusual. It's the dinner hour. People go inside to eat dinner, getting off the streets. Also, the thought of dinner is, I think, a palliative. A person who isn't feeling well and would drag himself or herself into the emergency room at almost any other hour of the day will think, "Well, maybe I'll feel better after dinner."

6:15 P.M.—Jim Blandsford calls, wanting to know whether I'm coming up to pediatrics. He tells me he's managed to save one slice of pizza for me, and Carrie's already into her mime act.

Things are quiet enough now in ER that I think it will be okay if I leave for a few minutes.

I hang up the phone, tell Calvin where I'm going, and say, "Call me if anything starts going on down here."

He gives me a wry look. "You know when you're not on duty, Sword, this place just literally folds."

As I step off the elevator on the seventh floor, Carrie is already in the middle of her performance. She does her mime act in the corridor of the pediatrics ward, which is shorter and wider than the one in the emergency room.

About a year ago, Jim persuaded a gifted painter among his volunteers (actually, Jim doesn't have volunteers, he has converts) to muralize the walls in the pediatrics corridor. There are clouds, trees, fences, buildings—but there aren't any kids in the murals.

"You see," Jim told me, "this way, the kids in the ward here can imagine themselves in the pictures any way they want."

The children who can stand or sit in wheelchairs line the sides of the corridor. The beds of the ones who aren't well enough to get up but are well enough to watch have been pushed to the doorways of their rooms. I see Nell, the girl with the kidney infection, in one.

Jim is sitting cross-legged on top of the counter of the nurses' station, a free-standing island that faces the elevators. He looks like an elf who's just dropped in from one of the murals.

As I stand near the elevator to watch Carrie's performance, I find myself thinking about Jim. He knows the birthdays of all the kids on this floor, how many brothers and sisters they have, and everything about their pets. That's the kind of relationship that develops in long-term care situations.

Most of my patients in ER stay only as long as it takes to treat them and send them home, or admit them into the hospital—so I've often wondered what it would be like to come to work and see the same patients day after day.

I've also wondered what it would be like to lose a patient, a child, whom you had grown close to over a long period of time.

I'm sure I couldn't do Jim's job, but at the same time I don't think he'd want to try mine either, because one day when ER was full of victims from a multiple car crash Jim said to me, "My God, sometimes you see more people die in one shift than I do in six months. How do you deal with that, Sword?"

Now as I look at these children who are watching Carrie, I recognize in their rapt faces the presence of the chronic diseases I don't have to deal with: cystic fibrosis, the leukemias, and other insidious forms of cancer that prey on them, and I am grateful for the diversity of ways people want to help one another.

The kids start to clap, and I focus on Carrie just in time to see her make the sweeping bow that ends her performance.

One of the nurses begins to pass around the wicker basket full of lollipops that marks the end of the evening, and Carrie comes over to where I'm standing. She wears a man's suit several sizes too large that she picked up in a Goodwill store, and a straw hat that looks as if a horse once sampled it for a snack.

"Maybe I should come downstairs and do my act in ER," she says. "If you're any criterion, I couldn't have a tougher audience."

"I'm sorry," I say, embarrassed.

"Bad day?"

"Not that bad. I guess I just have a lot on my mind."

"Oh. Something different, hm?" She uses such a wry tone, I'm startled. "Doctors," she says in answer to my look, "always have something on their minds. For instance, Jim and I can be sitting on a bluff above the ocean watching the sunset—you know, one of life's perfect moments— and I move closer waiting for him to say something intimate or touching or funny." She sighs. "And that's what I do, doctor, I wait."

I don't know whether to smile or not.

She goes on, "When I finally ask what's on his mind, I'm apt to get a quick rundown of the newest findings on sickle-cell anemia."

"That bad?" I say.

She shrugs. "I knew when I met Jim that all this . . ." she gestures at the ward, "would come first. And I thought I could handle it. The problem is I'm unnecessary here— where he really lives."

She makes a face. "Oh, well. I guess I'll give it another five years."

"You're doing great," I tell her, a little too heartily.

She glances across the room at Jim, who is listening intently as a child clutching a lollipop whispers something in his ear. He sees Carrie watching him, points at the clock above the elevator, and holds up five fingers.

"He thinks he means five minutes," she says, "but we'll be lucky if we're out of here in an hour."

"Yeah, well, I'd better be getting back to my own bailiwick," I say uneasily, and punch the down button.

The elevator doors open. I step in and turn around, and as the doors slide shut, Carrie tips her straw hat and waves. At that moment I wish she didn't remind me so much of Sandra.

6:43 P.M.—When I enter the white corridor, everything seems quiet. There aren't any charts with blue stickers in the chart rack.

Calvin is on the telephone, and I can tell from the expression on his face he's haranguing one of the clerks upstairs. As I draw near I hear him say, "Look, whatever you have to do to get him down here, do it. Otherwise, I will personally see to it that his next pay envelope contains a one-way ticket back to Lebanon."

I glance into the main treatment room, spotting Malone's and Alfred's feet beneath the curtain drawn around Mrs. Murphy's bed. I start to go in, hesitate, then am furious at myself for hesitating.

If it were any other doctor on my staff behind that curtain, I would approach without giving the matter a second thought. I realize I've started to put Malone's needs above those of a patient. And that's all it takes. I stride into the main treatment room and draw open the curtains.

Malone looks up from the chart he's writing on with an irritable glare, but I don't care. "How's she doing?" I ask.

He finishes writing on the treatment chart and shoves it at me. "Here!"

I scan the orders he has written; he's down to the

third drug of choice, but the drug he has chosen is correct. And then I do a double-take. He's written "1000 mg Pronestyl IV, push."

I hand the chart back to him. "Better double-check what you've written."

He gives me a furious look and barely glances at the chart. "My orders stand."

I don't believe what's happening. A thousand milligrams of Pronestyl would kill her.

"Michael," I say, "we don't give Pronestyl in boluses of a thousand. It has to be given in increments of one hundred up to a *maximum* of a thousand. Check the label."

He stares at me, realizing, at last, the magnitude of the error.

And just then, Calvin enters the treatment room.

"Dr. Sword, I've got an angry doctor at City Hospital on the phone. He wants to talk to the physician in charge here about Hattie Spencer."

Malone freezes for a second, extends the chart to me without a word, then continues out into the corridor.

I alter the orders on the chart, hand it to Alfred, and go out to the corridor to take the call at the nurses' station. "This is Dr. Sword."

"This is Dr. Miles in the ER at City. I don't know what the hell is going on at your place, but half an hour ago we admitted a thirteen-year-old girl in shock with a belly full of blood from a ruptured ectopic pregnancy. She went into full arrest during anesthesia, and we lost her. Her mother tells us she was in your ER this afternoon complaining of abdominal pain. Is that correct?"

"She left AMA," I say. There is nothing more I can say.

"Well, did you people examine her?"

"She would only submit to a partial," I reply.

"I see." He is silent then, but I can hear all the questions he isn't asking, the ones I would be asking if I were he.

"Well, okay, then." He hangs up. So do I. Malone is standing near the chart rack and asks, "What happened?"

I am so angry I scarcely trust myself to speak. "Ruptured ectopic pregnancy. She went into full arrest during preop."

He turns away very quickly so that I can't see his face.

"I want to talk to you in the doctors' room," I tell him grimly. I know this is it, that I have to let him go; but I have to give myself a minute.

He walks slowly down the corridor. I turn to Calvin and snap, "Did you get hold of Ahmad?" He knows my anger isn't directed at him. "He says he'll be right down."

I glance at the clock. It's 6:53. "Call him again," I say. "Tell him if he isn't here by six fifty-five, I will be up there to escort him personally."

Calvin nods. "My pleasure."

Then I walk down the corridor and turn into the doctors' room. It's empty.

I expect to find Malone in the driveway smoking a cigarette, but he isn't there. And when I walk across and look into the parking lot, his parking place is empty. I go back into the doctors' room and dial Sy's number.

"You caught me on my way out the door," he says. "What's up?"

"I have to cover the rest of Malone's shift."

"Oh? What happened?"

"I'll tell you when I see you. Want to have a late dinner tonight? Or make it tomorrow night?"

"Late is fine with me. Nine-thirty?"

"Okay. I'll see you at Russo's."

I go back out to the corridor just in time to see Dr. Ahmad coming out of the elevator. He smiles, but I don't smile back. I watch every step he takes and when he is in the main treatment room at Mrs. Murphy's bedside, I watch him there too, through the window at the nurses' station, until finally he pulls the curtain.

"Listen," Calvin says, "I was in a shop last week where they had these little voodoo dolls complete with pins. You want me to pick one up? I'll help you christen it Ahmad."

But this time even Calvin can't lighten my mood. I'll just be glad when this damn shift is over.

9:27 P.M.—I walk into Russo's, one of L.A.'s oldest restaurants. There aren't many places like it any more. At the far end there's a long, mahogany-topped bar with a brass rail running its full length. The mirror behind the bar is beveled. The Tiffany lamps above the tables are genuine, not imitations. Around the tables, the chairs are upholstered in crimson mohair and have substantial arms. The tables themselves are covered with damask cloths, and there are always fresh-cut flowers in the bud vases.

People who are serious about their need to relax come here. The light from the Tiffany lamps is soft. Conversations are held in low voices, as they are in an old, established club. As soon as you step in the door, you start to feel better.

I look around for Sy and spot him at the far end of the bar.

Paul, the bartender, nods a welcome when I take the stool next to Sy's and puts a glass of Heineken's in front of me, then discreetly goes away. I lift the beer to my lips and drink, feeling as if I may make it to tomorrow.

"So what happened?" Sy asks.

I give him a brief recap.

"Jesus. What are you going to do?"

"Let him go," I say. "I have no choice."

Sy stares into his glass. "Whatever made you want to be director anyway, Sword?"

"I don't know. Maybe it was the lights."

"What?"

"When I came to Los Angeles Memorial, we were working with outdated lights. I wanted the kind we had in the ER where I'd worked before. Reilly was director then, and I went to him and said, 'How about putting some new lights on the budget?' Well, he had other priorities. So when he resigned to go to San Diego and the directorship was up for grabs, I decided to try for it. And the first thing I did was buy some new lights."

"Um. Well, now that you've got your lights, what's in it for you?"

I grimace. "Power."

"That's not all."

"What do you mean?"

"I mean, I see you in that office, reviewing charts— how many every month?"

"I try to do five, maybe ten a day."

"And you work the night shift on just about every holiday that comes along because nobody else wants to, and if somebody has to miss a shift, you take it. That's not power, that's compulsion."

I shrug. "I don't care that much about holidays. Never did."

"And now you have to fire someone. Another fun thing a director gets to do."

"Yeah."

"Have you figured out what you're going to say to him?"

I shake my head.

"When are you going to do it?"

"Tomorrow. Before his shift starts."

We both stare at our glasses for a while, and I realize that Sy, like me, has been storing up worry for weeks about Malone. Probably we all have, because each of us is vulnerable to the same things that have pulled him down.

Suddenly Sy starts to speak about it. "You know, for all those years—medical school, internship, residency—we have to put off anything remotely resembling a normal life."

"I know."

"Yeah, hell, Dennis was telling me what they call the premed students at Loyola now. *Nerds.* I asked him what the definition of a nerd was, and he said a narrow, aggressive, anxiety-ridden, one-dimensional schmuck. That's what you turn into when you go after academic success to the exclusion of other values. And that's what you have to do to stand a chance of being accepted into medical school."

He's right. The MCAT (Medical College Admission Test) measures achievement in the basic sciences. And that's it. No history, no philosophy, no literature, no personal qualities.

"Good God, Sword," he continues, "by the time our apprenticeship is finally over, a lot of us are dying to turn back into human beings, have some fun, maybe make some mistakes. With Malone, it's been women—each one younger than the last, less suited to being a doctor's wife, and they've all taken a hunk out of him. The trouble is, he doesn't *learn.* When this marriage ends he'll be right out there at the end of the branch, and some little teenager will come along and pluck him off. If there's anything left to pluck, that is. You know what the suicide rate is in our profession?"

"No." And I'm not sure I want to.

"Well, it's damn high, and we contribute to it with our own brand of isolation."

I frown. "What do you mean?"

"Well, marriage for instance. Being a doctor certainly overrides our relationships with women. Doctors' wives aren't wives so much as they are accessories. And if the marriage ends, well, it's inconvenient as hell, but the core of our lives remains untouched. And that's just the beginning."

"Go on," I say.

"Well, doctors never really leave the fraternity. Once you become a doctor, you find yourself gravitating toward other doctors. If you attend a dinner party and there's another doctor there, guess who you end up talking to?

"If you have a wife, you encourage her, subtly at first, then not so subtly, to arrange social engagements with other doctors' wives. Doctors find each other on cruise ships, ski slopes, beaches; in hardware stores, barber shops, theater lobbies. Ultimately, the commonality of being a doctor overrides any other reason for friendship.

"And that means we've lost perspective; some of our good friends may be bad doctors, only we don't let ourselves acknowledge that, since we've begun to believe and then to perpetuate the myth that we're a special breed.

"Am I right? Who are you sitting with right now? And how many people do you see on a fairly frequent basis who aren't doctors?"

The answer to that, which I don't verbalize, is none. Even in my neighborhood, the only person I chat with regularly is an orthopedic surgeon who lives three houses down.

"Not that there isn't a good reason for it," Sy goes on. "Who else can understand us—or would want to?"

I trace the wet ring my glass has made on the bar. "So what's the answer?" I ask.

"I don't know," he replies. "But for Malone's sake— hell, for all of us—I hope there is one."

Then he shrugs. "Well, want to sit here and get drunk? That's one solution. Or should we move to a table and have dinner?"

"With what I've got ahead of me tomorrow," I say, "we'd better just have dinner."

"Right."

We get off the stools and head toward an empty table.

"Anything special planned for your Saturday with the girls?" Sy asks.

I shake my head.

"There's a Festival of the Masks in Hancock Park. Maybe they'd enjoy that."

"I'll think about it," I say.

But I know, and he knows, I won't be able to think about anything until I get past telling Malone that I have to let him go.

INTERLUDE

Friday

I wake up Friday morning exhausted.

All night long, or so it seemed (though Allen has told me dreams rarely take up more than one third of the time we spend sleeping) I was plagued by disturbing dreams I only remember snatches of now.

The segments that linger in my mind don't make any sense, so I push them out of my consciousness and turn my head toward the window.

Morning sunlight is illuminating the honeycombed pattern of the draperies. I lie still for several moments, knowing I don't have to get out of bed until noon if I don't want to.

Hell, what I want is for this day to be over with, to have the firing of Malone behind me.

Lying there, thinking about him, I realize I have never known anyone very well who has been fired. And I find it difficult to associate the concept of being fired with the concept of doctor. Clerks get fired; so do salesmen, cooks, and mechanics. Doctors may retire or change professions or die. They do not get fired.

And then I am remembering Josh Martin, the young ex-surgical resident looking for work who came in for an interview a few months ago.

During his second year as a surgical resident, searching for a way to cope with the stress he was under, Josh became addicted to Demerol.

Drug addiction takes its toll among doctors; nurses, too. It seems to prey on the best and the worst of us—those who barely passed their exams to squeeze through their internships, and those who were brilliant, whose names were always first on the list when exam scores were posted, those who were picked for the most coveted internships.

Josh was brilliant.

He was an incredibly appealing guy. With his sun-streaked hair and deeply tanned skin he looked like a surfer, except that, close up, his face had too many lines.

He was candid about his experience. "I didn't wait to get caught," he said. "I stopped myself. Resigned my residency and entered a detox program. Gave myself six months to mellow out, find myself again. And now—I'm ready to go back to work."

I liked Josh Martin. And when there was an opening on the staff, I thought about hiring him. I told myself the only reason I didn't was because I felt he should go back into surgery; that that had been the specialty he had chosen, and that I didn't want a doctor on my staff for whom emergency medicine was an expedient second choice.

But the real reason was, I felt I couldn't take the risk. The Humpty Dumpty syndrome. You're just never sure, once someone falls apart under the pressures of the medical profession, that they can ever, really, be put back together again.

Well, I know if I lie here any longer, I will *never* leave this bed.

So I get up, pull back the draperies, open the sliding door, and step out onto the small enclosed patio brilliant with morning sunlight. I stand there for a moment, stretching and breathing deeply; then I go back into the bedroom and start to put on my sweats, my jogging shoes. I will run the four miles I always run on days when I don't have to go to the hospital. Then I will come home and have breakfast (foregoing the chocolate ice cream drenched in chocolate syrup I used to have for breakfast on my days off, but which, Sandra told me, was terrible for my cholesterol level). Instead I will fix fresh-squeezed orange juice, toast, eggs.

What I'm trying to do, of course, is focus my thoughts on any small thing that will serve as a buffer zone to get me through the beginning of this day.

But as I leave the house and start the first lap of my four-mile route, one of the things Sy said to me last night lingers in my mind. "Sword, you ever get the feeling your life is haunted? That even in the time we're not being doctors, we're still being doctors?"

I can be doing so mundane a thing as trimming the yew hedge in my back yard when some pattern of light or shadow will send my thoughts back to the hospital, and the faces of the patients will surface.

Or else I find myself thinking about staff or about a piece of equipment I know we must have or—it goes on and on.

I asked Allen once if he carried his work inside him

everywhere he went, and he said, "Yes, of course I do. I think anyone whose profession is allied to helping people probably does that. But if I'm going to be in the best possible shape for my patients during the hours I devote to them, then the rest of my life has to be free. It wasn't easy for me to accept this, Randy. And it isn't going to be easy for you, either."

I know he's right. But can I segregate my thoughts and feelings into doctor and nondoctor compartments? I just don't know whether it's possible for me *not* to be compulsive about my profession.

As I leave the house, I lift my face to the morning sunlight, feeling the cool breeze off the Pacific. I will myself to be conscious of the movement of my legs, to concentrate on taking smooth, rhythmic strides, breathing deeply, filling my mind with the sensation of running.

I pass other joggers. Most are the same ones I see whenever I run at this time; a few of them nod, say "Good morning." It's okay, I think, to permit them into my sphere of awareness as I concentrate on running.

I see an attractive woman with ash-blonde hair running toward me. She runs beautifully, in a perfect rhythm. I envy those who make running look totally effortless (I am not one of them yet).

As she draws near she smiles, and I smile back; but when she is past me I am remembering the woman the police brought in early last Saturday morning.

All the beds were empty, the night's casualties had been attended to, and I was thinking it had been one of my easier nights in ER—when the police car pulled up to the ambulance entrance. Two officers walked through the sliding doors with a woman who was wearing a grass- and mud-stained jogging suit and one of those beaded Indian bands around her head. There was a large, ugly bruise on her right cheek; her eye was swollen shut.

While Illana helped get her settled in the examining room, I talked in the corridor with the police, and they told me she had been raped. There weren't many people in the street at that hour, they said, and another unit close to the scene had caught the man.

She was determined to press charges, to have the man brought to trial. She had asked to be driven to the emergency room because she wanted the rape to be corroborated by an examining physician and to have the evidence collected. If necessary, she wanted me to appear in court.

It was, she had told the police, the second time she had been raped. The first time she had told no one, done nothing.

I remember when I went into the examining room how her whole body was clenched in anger. I told her the examination would be much easier if she would relax, and she tried, but she couldn't.

I wonder if I will be called to testify in court on her behalf. I've done it before, in other rape cases . . . and my mind begins to replay the last one.

MR. JONES: Dr. Sword, you were the emergency room physician on duty at Los Angeles Memorial Hospital on the night of August 7th?

A I was.

Q You examined the plaintiff?

A I did.

Q You found physical evidence on the plaintiff's body to corroborate her statement that she was raped?

A I did.

Q Would you please describe the evidence that you found?

A I found friction burns on her inner thighs; I found tears in the internal genital area, also bruises and lacerations on her lower torso; lacerations on her throat where the knife held by the assailant penetrated the skin.

MR. SMITH: Objection. Assumes facts not in evidence. Please instruct the witness to confine his testimony to what he himself witnessed.

LAW JUDGE: Objection sustained.

MR. JONES: Dr. Sword, did you find any laboratory evidence that would corroborate the plaintiff's contention that she had been raped?

A I did.

Q Would you please describe that evidence?

A I found several strands of hair entangled in her pubic hair that were not hers. She had, clutched in her hand when the police brought her in, a piece of cloth, which my nurse pried out of her fingers and which she said she had torn from the man's shirt.

Damn it, I am supposed to be concentrating on running.

Well, I've run two miles. I will run the last two and think about its being autumn.

The colors of the leaves here don't spread across the spectrum of orange, yellow, and red as they do in Pennsylvania. And yet, I never thought about the colors of the leaves when I was growing up there. A professor of philosophy from USC whose broken finger I splinted told me that was the plight of Western man, that we rarely inhabit the present moment; with us, it's always yesterday or tomorrow.

I see the bald man ahead who runs with his Doberman, and as usual, as soon as he sees me, he calls the dog to his side and clips on its leash, and as I pass by him he glares at me. I could understand his hostility if this were the first time I had ever encountered him, and he perhaps believed he had established the pattern of having the street to himself at this particular time of day; but three out of five times that I run I encounter this man, and it's almost like a dance step we go through.

Ah well, do not look gift horses in the mouth, I tell myself. I am grateful that he leashes his dog. I have seen and treated so many varieties of bites—dog bites, cat bites, horse bites, hamster bites, human bites (the nastiest and most prone to infection of all)—but . . .

I have a mile to go.

Well, damn it, I can't think only about running. Should I think about Waldo? Waldo used to run with me. He was a golden retriever, and ten years old when I first started to run. He hadn't been exercised enough in his lifetime, and he was too fat. But he and I managed to get in shape together until we could run four miles. After we had been running for a while, he began taking his own side trips away from the route I followed, and I would see his tail, like the plume on a courtier's hat, appearing in the tall grass ahead of me, or wafting through somebody's flower garden.

Waldo didn't understand when Sandra and Tod and the girls moved out of the house. He was bewildered, living alone with me, waiting for me to come home, watching me sleep when I did, seldom receiving any table scraps. Nor did he understand the rage that formed the fabric of most of my moods immediately following the divorce. In fact, he was so confused (and yes, he had, by then, twelve years on him, a good number for a dog) that he died. But his ghost haunts my house. A lot of the time, I think I see him when he isn't there.

Alexis, I'm sure, blames me for Waldo's death. In her

six-year-old intuitive way, she senses there was more than old age involved in his dying. She also wonders, since I am a doctor, why I didn't fix him.

Sad thoughts to be thinking when I am supposed to be concentrating on the joy of running.

I see the fence of my house ahead and I congratulate myself on one thing. I did manage, during the entire time that I was running, not to think about Malone.

I jog through the front door into my living room, do a few stretch-outs while I cool down, go into the kitchen and start the coffee maker, then head for the shower.

I am a cliché in the shower. I sing—a lot, and badly. And when I have a particularly thorny problem confronting me, I think about it while I'm standing under a warm jet of water.

So I let myself think, now, about Malone. It's almost a relief not to keep trying to push thoughts about him away. I've decided I'm going to call Allen, ask him if I can come and talk to him. I think he'll let me if he has an hour free. I know Allen isn't going to be able to tell me what to say to Malone. But he will listen to me outline the problem, allow me to express my doubts, my panic. And afterward, I hope I will have a clearer perspective. That is what talking with Allen usually does for me.

It is so damned ironic, because I fought going to him, point blank refused when Sandra first broached the subject, which was long before she started talking about divorce.

"Our marriage will be fine," I told her, though I did admit, "I know I'm tired, and yes, I don't spend enough time with you and the children. But that's all going to change as soon as I get this directorship under my belt and finish the research I started on ER thoracotomies and find a new assistant director and revamp the budget."

What a plan. A year later Sandra left, and that's when I started going to Allen. After it was all over.

However, I realize my going to see Allen marks the first time in my life since my father's death that I am willing to consider the idea that I, Randall Sword, might need help.

My father died when I was sixteen. All the time I was growing up he was a commander in the naval reserve. I think he treated me much as he treated the midshipmen under him—expecting me, always, to be more than I was ready to be: my behavior and grades were never good enough; my athletic prowess also fell short of his mark. The list of my faults was long.

When he died, I experienced a single sharp moment of relief that was almost like an electric shock. Guilt-ridden, I carry the ghost of him around inside my head and give life to that ghost, sometimes, with Tod—treating him the same way my father treated me.

I'm beginning to understand these things now.

Allen is helping me learn to cope, too, with my belief that, like my father, I am going to die at midlife. He died when he was fifty-two. I know I won't fully rid myself of this ghost until I have passed my fifty-second birthday.

By the time I towel off and shave, the coffee is done. I glance at the clock. Allen should be in his office now. I dial his number. He says his schedule is full up, but if I'd like to bring a sandwich along, I can brown-bag it with him. I say I'll see him at noon, and hang up.

But I find I can't eat breakfast, not toast, not anything. I can't even drink more than half a cup of coffee. I know I won't be able to eat anything until I've spoken to Malone. Until then, my stomach won't be able to handle food.

I have a couple of hours to fill, so I begin to plan my

day tomorrow with the girls. I think Sy's suggestion about the Festival of the Masks is a good one. I like the thought of taking them into the city, because they lead such insulated lives. That is what Sandra and I decided we wanted for them when we moved into a safe, upper-middle-class neighborhood. The house Sandra rented is in a similar neighborhood. But something is missing in such places, something to do with life's urgency that I experience in the white corridor.

It almost comes down to an equation. If everything is as safe and easy as it is in Palos Verdes, what becomes important? It's a subject that's been on my mind lately, and I need to talk to someone about it—maybe Sy, maybe Allen . . . maybe even Sandra.

My newspaper is advertising the Festival of the Masks, so I make a call and find out the time and route of the parade. When I hang up, I realize how much I'm looking forward to tomorrow. And how important it is to have something to look forward to.

When I enter Allen's office, he is just spreading out his lunch on the desk. Allen is a substantial man, not tall but with large bones, and he is, as he says, "well fleshed out." His hair is graying at the temples, and his whiskers are so dense that even an hour after shaving his face is shadowed.

I'm still not hungry, but I stopped at a patisserie and picked up two Napoleons and two containers of coffee. He eyes the bakery box with interest.

"A bribe?" he asks.

The tone of his voice isn't exactly jocular, but I decide to take his comment lightly. "Fee for service," I reply.

He doesn't smile.

Hell, I think, I probably shouldn't have come. I know how I feel when I can't even have twenty minutes for lunch to myself. And then I start to get a little irritated. If he didn't want to give up his lunch hour, he shouldn't have volunteered to see me.

"Well," he says, "tell me about it."

With surprising difficulty, I begin to describe what happened with Malone last night. Allen listens intently as he eats his turkey sandwich, a gigantic dill pickle, two deviled eggs, and one of the Napoleons.

I push the second one across the desk to him.

When I've finally told him everything, he says, "So, what is it?"

I frown. "What do you mean?"

"I mean, the man alienated a critically ill patient to the point where she wouldn't let him treat her, made a grave error in writing orders for medication, then walked off his shift. Why didn't you call him at home last night and tell him not to bother coming back? Or send him a telegram? Why are you putting yourself through this?"

"I—I don't know."

"I think you do."

I am beginning to wish I had taken that second Napoleon and shoved it in his face. "Remind me never to infringe on your lunch hour again," I say.

"Randy."

"What?"

"There is no easy way to fire a man."

"I know that."

"Why did you come here?"

"Because I feel lousy. I can't eat, for chrissake. I feel like I've been kicked in the stomach by a camel."

"Okay," he says. "What if you were firing the janitor?"

"What?"

"You have a janitor or a custodian, don't you?"

"Yeah."

"Well, what if he did something stupid and dangerous —like, I don't know, leaving some infectious waste around where it could endanger patients?"

"I'd fire him on the—" I stop. "Well, that's different."

"Why?"

"A janitor is different from a doctor."

"How different?"

"I mean, he didn't spend eight goddamn years of his life learning how to be a janitor, for one thing."

"Are you suggesting that a lengthy education entitles a person to make a certain number of mistakes?"

"No," I say heatedly, "not at all."

"Then what are you saying?"

"That I'm sorry as hell for the man."

"Are you so sorry for him you're not going to fire him?"

"No."

"Do you remember what your first reaction was last night when you learned the girl had died?"

I frown. "Rage."

"Okay. And then?"

I close my eyes, going back to that moment. I remember wanting him to . . . to say something; say he was sorry; anything. And when he didn't, I remember thinking about his irritability with me when I entered the room where he was treating the girl; also that before he saw the girl, he was worried about Mrs. Murphy; the fact that Dr. Ahmad was impossibly slow in getting down to ER, and that because there were no beds available upstairs in either ICU or CCU the patient had to be stabilized in ER, and

Malone had had to assume responsibility for a patient much longer than he should have.

In short, I was looking for excuses. But they didn't help.

I tell Allen all this, and he is silent.

I continue, "You know, Malone and I are alike in some ways. We're both doctors, divorced, about the same age. We were near the top of our class in medical school and we're both obsessed with medicine. Jesus, I think he even has a dog that died recently." My words are coming fast now; I'm getting close to something. "You know, after the mess of two divorces, then paying alimony to women who don't love you any more, plus being a compulsive worker, well, what if one day even the hospital starts closing in? There'd be nowhere to turn. I might—Jesus, Allen, maybe I could get as close to the edge as Malone."

Allen nods. "So Malone has become a kind of dark looking-glass through which you can see yourself some day?"

I think that one over, and then say, "It's possible. If things go badly. Yes. Firing Malone, it's like I'm firing myself, or some future threatened self."

"Does knowing that help?" Allen asks.

"I think so," I say. "Some, at least." I wish suddenly I could go on with this, find out more, but I glance at the clock. Allen's lunch hour is just about over.

I say, "If I knew who your next patient was going to be, I'd bribe him, or her, to be late."

Allen shrugs and gives me a half smile. "I'll see you at your usual Monday time?"

"Sure."

"Call me before then, if you need to."

"Right." Reluctant to leave, I watch him spread the

morning paper out on his desk; then, without a good-bye, I leave the office.

Going down in the elevator, I wonder if I should call Malone or just show up at his door. I've never been to his apartment, but I copied down his address last night. He lives in Marina Del Rey, which is about half an hour from here.

The marina's town houses facing the boat slips are white imitation stucco with blue imitation-tile roofs. There are tall wrought-iron street lamps along the walkways that have fake lanterns on top. The grass growing in the spaces between the walkways is real, but it is so closely and neatly trimmed, it looks like an outdoor carpet.

In the boat slips, the boats are all blue and white, freshly painted, bobbing up and down.

Slightly nauseated, I avert my eyes.

Marina Del Rey probably isn't a bad place to live. It's the kind of place I might have lived in in my twenties. But not, I think, in my forties. Not even if I had a teenage wife. Sy says Malone is way past caring where he lives. Few of us have met Wife Number 3, although Sy has. He says she's lovely to look at and that's all he knows, because she's kept her guard up whenever he's been around. She met Malone playing volleyball on the beach one day. They got married the week after she graduated from high school, two years ago.

The picture of her that has emerged from the ER gossip is that she spends her days the same way she would have spent them if she hadn't married Malone (playing volleyball on the beach, watching television), the most significant difference in her life being that Malone is picking up the tab instead of her parents; also that she is no longer, apparently, planning to go to college, although she was when Malone first met her.

Spinnaker Way is the name of the street they live on. Their house is 301B Spinnaker Way.

What if Mrs. Malone answers the door? Suddenly I have this picture of a nubile young redhead in a string bikini standing on the threshold. What can I say to her?

And then, straight ahead of me, the street marker comes into view—Spinnaker Way. And moments later I am staring at brass numerals on a blue door: 301B.

I ring the bell. The door is opened by a pleasant-looking girl with reddish-brown hair and a generous sprinkling of freckles across the bridge of her nose. Her large brown eyes are too young to have circles under them, but there's something about her expression that makes me think she's working on them. She's wearing a halter and shorts; the halter has several food stains on it, and she's holding a large wooden spoon.

I have an unerring nose for chocolate, which I smell now. I can often distinguish, by scent, not only what variety it is, but what is being done with it. Mrs. Malone is baking chocolate chip cookies.

I ask her, "Is M-M-M-Michael home?" Damn it! Not now.

"He is," she replies, politely ignoring the stutter. "But he's asleep. I don't like to wake him unless it's important." She gives me a small, almost conspiratorial smile. "He's a doctor."

"I'm afraid it is important," I say spacing my words.

The expression in her eyes is puzzled, troubled. "Are you a friend of Michael's?"

"I'm sorry. I should have introduced myself. I'm Randall Sword."

"Oh, gosh," she says, then is embarrassed at having said it, and we just stand there until she backs a few steps into the room and says, "Please, come in."

I follow her, wishing I were an insurance salesman or a Fuller Brush man.

A buzzer is buzzing somewhere, and we're both aware of it at the same moment.

"Excuse me," she exclaims softly, then disappears through an open archway into a kitchen that I can see from here has blue and white wallpaper, anchors and boats.

I hear her open an oven door, and the melting chocolate smell grows stronger.

In a few minutes, she returns. She's carrying a white paper napkin with three cookies on it, which she holds out to me. "Michael told me once how much you like chocolate."

I smile and murmur, "Thank you," and take the cookies from her, wondering, how I can accept cookies baked by the wife of a man I am about to fire?

It's obvious how much she wishes I would go away. She knows my having come here is ominous.

"Sit down, please. I'll go tell Michael you're here."

She leaves the room as I sit on the edge of a denim-covered couch, grateful to be alone. I put the cookies on the coffee table in front of the couch and rub my palms on my pants; then I look around the room.

I went to a party once in a house Michael owned in Westwood when he was married to his second wife. "Elegant" was the word Sandra used to describe everything inside it—the wicker furniture, the signature prints on the walls, the distressed pine table in the dining room; also Michael's then-wife, who was skinny and had frizzy hair and huge eyes and wore, Sandra said, "incredible clothes."

Until this moment, I didn't even know I remembered that evening.

In contrast to that living room this one certainly isn't elegant, but it's much more lived in. The magazines on the coffee table next to my napkin of cookies have the look of having been thoroughly read. There's cat hair or dog hair, I can't tell which, on the couch I'm sitting on. ("Good," I think, "maybe his dog didn't die after all.") I see a half-finished piece of macrame on the denim-upholstered chair that matches the couch. A comfortable-looking Irish knit sweater hangs on a coat tree near the front door I just walked through.

The room isn't what I expected. The girl isn't either.

What I expected was a trendy apartment full of Plexiglas with a Lolitalike wife, which would have made—although I don't know exactly why—what I am about to do a little easier.

Mrs. Malone comes back into the room and says, "Michael will be out in just a minute." She sits down then, on the edge of the overstuffed chair, picks up the unfinished piece of macrame, fingering it absently. Her voice is small, uncertain. "Has something happened?"

I shift my position uneasily, but before I can answer, she goes on. "Michael—well, Michael's been awfully tired lately. He works too hard. I keep trying to talk him into taking a vacation—you know, maybe even as much as a couple of months." She pauses, but there is nothing I can think of to say. So she continues, "He tells me, 'Jill, we can't afford a vacation.' But I've been doing some craft projects that are starting to bring in a little money, and I think we could. Mexico's not too expensive."

She pauses again and I realize she's trying to ask me to tell Michael to take a leave of absence. But ER contracts aren't set up to accommodate leaves. By gerrymandering the shift schedule, I can arrange to give someone as much as twenty days off—only that's not enough to help Michael.

Now there is silence between us until I say inanely, "A vacation would be nice."

She knows I have rejected her request, but surprisingly there is no hostility in the look she gives me, simply acceptance of her defeat. "Excuse me," she says softly, places the macrame on the chair and goes into the kitchen.

A minute or two passes before Michael enters the room carrying a mug of steaming coffee. He sits down in the chair where the macrame is, puts the mug on the coffee table, and the macrame on the rug. He eyes the cookies I have left there uneaten, then looks at me for the first time. "Want some coffee?"

The last time I was offered refreshment in a tense situation (when I was meeting with the hospital board members trying to get them to expand the bed capacity of the ER from fourteen to twenty beds), I refused the offer, then sensed I had committed a faux pas—thereby learning a lesson. Being offered and accepting refreshments shows an openness on both sides—if not to negotiate, then to be willing to share something.

So I say, "Yes, thank you," to the coffee I know I won't be able to drink.

Michael gets up and goes into the kitchen. He's wearing a plaid cotton shirt, jeans, and spattered mellow loafers that he and I, in better days, had joked about: "Hey, Sword, I bet I've got more Type A on my left shoe than you have on both of yours."

Damn! What did I have to look at his shoes for?

He comes back, carrying the coffee mug carefully in both hands, and sets it on the table in front of me. Then he sits down again in the overstuffed chair. He hasn't taken the time to shave and looks as if he didn't sleep well, but then he's looked that way for weeks.

Jill Malone comes into the room from the kitchen and says to Michael, "I'm going for a walk. There's plenty more coffee—and cookies if you want some." Then she takes the cardigan off the coat tree and goes out the front door.

"Nice lady, Michael," I say softly.

He nods and picks up his coffee cup. "Deserves better."

It wasn't a specious remark; he doesn't expect to be argued with.

And I have to get on with what I've come to do.

"Michael," I say, "I have to let you go."

He doesn't reply, doesn't seem to move at all, but the coffee mug he's holding in his right hand suddenly wobbles, spilling coffee onto the table. Slowly, he brings his left hand over to take the mug, then he sets it down.

"I don't understand what's happened to me." He looks at me. "I was a good doctor, Sword. You know I was."

"Yes," I say. "I know that."

"How could it all go so wrong, get so damned insane?" His eyes have that terrible hunted look I would see sometimes in the white corridor.

"Michael, maybe—"

He cuts me off. "No. There are no maybes. It's all gone."

I don't think I've ever heard that tone of finality in anybody's voice before.

He stands up. "Thank you for coming. I mean—for not telling me on the phone. Or at the hospital. But if you don't mind, I'd like to be alone now."

I want to say something gentle, even encouraging, but there isn't anything.

I do pause at the door and turn to look at him. "You can get well, Michael. I know you can."

He doesn't respond to that, so I open the door and step into sunlight so bright it hurts my eyes.

Walking back to my car, I look for Jill Malone, but I don't see her.

I'm halfway back to Palos Verdes before I start to cry. I just take the first off ramp I see, pull onto a quiet side street, and let the tears come.

INTERLUDE

Saturday

Saturday morning.

I wake at dawn and cannot get back to sleep. Even after I've run my four miles and showered and had breakfast, it's only 8:30.

I meant to call Sandra last night and ask her whether she could drive into L.A. late this afternoon to pick up the girls so that I could go directly to the hospital after the festival. But I fell asleep in front of the TV a little while after I got home, and when I finally roused myself enough to go to bed, it was too late to call her.

Now it's probably too early.

She used to like to sleep late on Saturday mornings. Alexis and Vanessa would wake up between six and seven (Tod was a typically late-sleeping adolescent), and when they got tired of playing (or fighting) with each other, or watching Saturday-morning cartoons, they would come into our room—sometimes singly, sometimes together—

wanting food, or comfort, or an adult to play with; or all three.

If I weren't going to the hospital that Saturday, Sandra would bury her head beneath the pillows and I would hoist a daughter under each arm and amble out to the kitchen. Not a bad way to start the weekend.

I don't know what Sandra's Saturday mornings are like now. Many aspects of her life that were once familiar to me aren't any more. She is living in a new neighborhood, has put the girls in nursery school and kindergarten, and has taken a part-time job.

Yet the skeletal structure of my own life remains much the same. I go to the hospital; I come home and rest, then return to the hospital. It is "the inner man," Allen tells me, that is undergoing metamorphosis.

Maybe he's right. Once upon a time I wouldn't have given a second thought to waking Sandra. Now, I worry about it.

I busy myself with chores to pass the time: adjust the mechanism on the garage door opener; put a new washer in the bathroom showerhead; replace the filter in the fish pond; hose off the car. I wish the girls were with me as I do these things. They've spent a few such Saturdays watching me putter around, and I think they find it comforting.

They were so shy with me in the house immediately following the divorce. Well, who could blame them? For a time I know they felt like displaced persons, wondering which house, this one or their mother's, was really theirs. I could see it in their eyes, the tentative way they walked into the living room on their first visits.

But the more time they spent with me here, the more they understood that I was not going to leave and that their room, with their possessions inside it, would remain intact.

Alexis, especially, seems to crave my "fix-it" sessions. She will hunt earnestly for things that need to be repaired, and will bring them to me, or take me to them. What she really wants, of course, is for the two halves of what was once her life to be put back together again.

By the time I've finished with the fish pond filter, it's a little after nine, and I decide it's okay to call Sandra. Tod answers the phone. There is a moment of strained silence before I ask how he is. He says, "Fine." More silence. I ask him if his mother is up yet. He says, "I'll see," and a minute later Sandra comes on the line.

I can tell from the testiness in her voice that she thinks I am calling to cancel my day with the girls. I have never done that, but for some reason she always thinks I will. I suppose because she felt so deserted before our marriage ended, she still believes in the old patterns that governed our lives.

I tell her I want to take the girls into L.A. to the Festival of the Masks and ask her if she would be willing to drive in and pick them up. On sudden impulse, which I know I shouldn't give in to because I haven't taken the time to think it through, I say, "We could have an early dinner together, the four of us. Tod, too, if he'd like to come."

After a beat of silence she says, "I don't think dinner would be a good idea. But I don't mind driving in for the girls."

"Fine," I say. "Why don't you meet us on the steps of the museum at five?"

She agrees, and we say good-bye.

Do I feel rejected, or relieved? Relieved, I decide. Not enough time has passed for us to be able to have dinner together. Maybe some day . . .

I am in a fairly good mood when I leave the house

half an hour later. The weather is still fine—cool, crisp, and clear here, though it will probably be fifteen degrees warmer in the city.

The man who lives across the street is out pruning his rosebushes. On impulse, I wave as I drive by. He gives me a startled look (I am the scowling doctor who never waves), and I am almost at the end of the block before he lifts his hand and waves back.

It's a half-hour drive to Sandra's. The girls are excited when I arrive. With Vanessa it takes the form of nonstop sentences spilling over each other: What is a festival? What kinds of masks will there be? Who will be wearing them? With Alexis, the excitement is all in her eyes, the pink flush on her cheekbones.

I have never been inside this house they live in. Sandra always has them ready and waiting and brings them to meet me at the door. Over Sandra's shoulder I see Tod standing at the end of the hallway, but when he sees me, he quickly disappears.

Sometimes I think this breach between Sandra and me has wounded him more than anyone—both by virtue of his being a teenager and because he has had no contact with his natural father. We adopted each other, as father, as son. I am tempted now to stride into the house, seize Tod by the shoulders, and demand that he stop hiding from me—which I know would be a mistake. Then I hear Sandra murmur softly, "He just needs more time," and I look at her in surprise. It is the gentlest thing she has said to me in months. I think she is surprised herself. She starts fussing with the barrettes in Alexis's hair.

She is a pretty woman, my ex-wife. Shoulder-length dark chestnut hair, large, expressive brown eyes, a generous mouth, skin the color of buttermilk. We met in the hospital in Panama where I did my internship. She was working there as an x-ray technician, supporting herself and Tod. We returned to the States at the same time, lived together for a while, and then decided to get married. We were such good friends. There are a lot of things I miss about our marriage, but most of all, I think, the friendship.

Vanessa is skipping in impatient circles around me, and Alexis is watching me anxiously. I'd better leave while I'm ahead. I take the girls by the hand, reaffirming to Sandra, "Five o'clock then, in front of the museum?"

"I'll be there."

Vanessa is, as always, rambunctious, positioning her body in an endless and astonishing variety of positions in the back seat, filling the car with nonstop chatter ("Guess who threw sand at me last Thursday . . . Do you want to know the color of Mommy's new lipstick? . . . Tod likes his new school better than his old one because he's the best tennis player in this one . . ."). I sometimes wonder if she feels a sense of obligation to fill in what she perceives as the empty spaces left by her sister's silences.

Initially, I am responsive—even grateful for her ebullience. But by the time we reach the outskirts of L.A., my mood has taken a downward swing. I wonder if it's because we're drawing close to the hospital. My thoughts, despite all the admonitions Allen has instilled in me and despite my willing them not to, seem determined to focus there the closer we come to it. Well, I will not let them. I insert a tape into the stereo of the Limelighters singing children's songs. Within seconds, Vanessa is singing happily along; then I join in; and so, finally, does Alexis. We become our own parade. People passing in the fast lane point and smile and we smile back.

I am wishing we could continue moving through time and space this way, and whatever automatic thing it is in me that takes over each time I make the drive between my house and Los Angeles Memorial takes over now. I exit at the Juniper Street off-ramp, even though that is not the most direct route to Hancock Park and not the one I intended to take. Now we are only minutes away from the hospital. Abruptly, I stop singing; seconds later so does Alexis; and as the tape clicks off, so does Vanessa. I expect her to ask me to turn it over and play the other side, but she doesn't; she is quiet.

The girls have never seen Los Angeles Memorial, don't know it's just ahead, or what happened, why silence overtook us. I could drive right on by and not say anything.

But suddenly I'm damned if I will. Lord knows what they've fashioned in their minds from listening to Sandra and me quarrel about "that place."

So I point to it out the window and say, "See, girls, that's where I work."

Alexis's hands, I notice, clench in her lap and she turns her head slowly as if she expects to see a behemoth looming alongside the car.

I glance at Vanessa in the rear-view mirror. She is frowning intently out the window. "You mean that big tan building with all the little windows?" I have never thought of it that way, but she is right. "Uh-huh."

"It's bigger than your last hospital," she pronounces.

I didn't even know she remembered the hospital in Redondo Beach.

"Yes," I agree, "it is."

Alexis's hands have relaxed. "Where's your emergency place?"

I circle around the block and point out the emergency entrance where the ambulances pull up. One is parked there now, but its lights aren't flashing. Could be the crew has just stopped by to replenish their supplies.

"Some day," I say, "I'll give you a tour."

I half expect Vanessa to say, "Now, Daddy!" But she doesn't. Perhaps she intuits, as I do, it's better to take one small step at a time. I continue up Juniper Street and turn left on Wilshire. It's 11:30, and the parade is scheduled to pass by Hancock Park at noon. By the time we arrive there, park, and find a place to stand with the crowd lining the sidewalk, we can hear the sound of a marching band in the distance.

Vanessa cannot be still. Even Alexis gives a little hop-step as she tries to stand quietly next to me. The sun is warm on the top of our heads. The sky is incredibly blue. There is a wonderful sense of expectancy in the air. A fleet of what appears to be a hundred, maybe two hundred helium-filled balloons tied together is released into the sky, and the wind currents sculpt them into shapes that change constantly as we watch.

"It's a snake," Vanessa exclaims. "No, no, a dragon."

"It's a magic balloon carpet," Alexis says softly, "on its way to the cloud princess."

And even as I am enjoying their enjoyment, I am hoping the children on Jim's ward in the hospital are watching the balloons, too, out the windows of their room.

The girls have seen parades before, but not like this one. Today, besides the requisite high-school marching bands and majorettes and baton twirlers, there are Chinese dragons, Indonesian temple dancers, a Japanese drum-and-flute corps, a marimba band, Samoan fireaters, and a troop of Rasta singers—most of them wearing extraordinary masks. For once in her life, Vanessa's expectations of what an event should be are met, and Alexis is enchanted, even awed.

The marchers in the parade turn into Hancock Park, an intriguing area that houses the County Art Museum, the La Brea Tar Pits, and the George C. Page Museum. I have never taken the girls to any of these places. Since the divorce we've gone on endless excursions to the beach, camping in the mountains, and skiing at Big Bear, but I have not explored this city with them.

We cross Wilshire and follow the last of the parade performers into the park, where booths and stages have been set up. A figure wearing a hawk-faced mask and wings of crimson silk leaps out at us from behind a tree. Vanessa shrieks with delight, though Alexis regards the creature thoughtfully.

The winged figure leaves us to become part of a passing chain of dancers. When the last person in the chain holds out a beckoning hand, I think all three of us are tempted to join; but we're also starving—and the smells from the food booths are irresistible. We move from one to the next to the next, slowly, sampling everything—sushi, teriyaki, empanadas, quesadillas, satay kambing madura. I see all the shades of skin here I see in the white corridor—but there is no pain, no anger in the faces. This is a celebration.

When we've finally tasted everything, we stroll among the booths where the masks are on display. There are masks from Mexico, Japan, Korea, Africa; from several North American Indian tribes—Navajo, Hopi, Kwakiutl; fantasy masks made in Hollywood.

Fingering the wood of one mask, I remember, suddenly, the main street running through Addis Abbaba, where on any given day you might see Beni Amer herdsmen, turbaned Christian holy men, richly shawled Moslem girls, Anuak villagers adorned with ivory and the hair of giraffe tails.

There is something intoxicating about being in the middle of several different cultures. That is one hold on me I know the white corridor has.

I'm glad I brought the girls here, pleased they are seeing L.A.'s wonderful mix of cultures at its best. When I do take them to visit the white corridor—and I will—they will probably see pain, anger, and suffering, but they will also have the memory of this.

I tell them both they can choose a mask to take home.

Vanessa picks a purple and pink Hollywood fantasy mask glittering with sequins. Alexis lingers over her choice, then finally selects a hinged hawk-face mask that opens to reveal a child's face inside.

Our shadows begin to lengthen on the grass. The chill of autumn that has been delayed by the October sun is growing stronger. I look at my watch for the first time since we entered the park—almost five o'clock. There are more people leaving now than arriving, and I tell the girls it's time to go and meet their mother. We are all quiet as we walk out of the park.

On the steps of the museum, Sandra is standing in a square of sunlight that has no warmth to it. She is wearing a blue wool cardigan, and she holds the collar together at her throat. I look at her almost as I would a stranger: who is she waiting for, this pretty woman with tired eyes? She smiles when she sees the girls.

Vanessa lets go of my hand and runs up the steps, trying to tell her mother every single thing that happened during the entire day.

Alexis continues to hold on to my hand, but I know that inside she, too, is letting go. Saying good-bye to any-one at any time is hard for her. She will, I know, tell Sandra about her day during the ride home, when Vanessa is sound asleep in the back seat.

I move toward Sandra, and as soon as Vanessa lets me get a word in, I say, "Thanks for driving up here."

"It worked out well," she replies. "Tod is spending

the night at a friend's, and I drove in early enough so that I could go to the museum. It's been a long time since I've done that."

I'm aware now of how cut off—perhaps stranded is a better word—Sandra felt during the first few years after the girls were born. She had Tod when she was in her early twenties. To take on the role of mothering babies in her late thirties was more demanding than either of us realized it would be. And I was damn little help. Now I think Sandra is in the process of learning how to reclaim her life. I wish I could tell her how much I wish her well. But all I can do is murmur, "Yes, well, that's good."

Why do I feel so awkward with her? Well, I think she does with me, too.

She plunges her hands into the pockets of her cardigan. "We'd better be on our way."

I'm tempted to renew my invitation to dinner. But I know how tired the girls are, and instead I hear myself saying, "I had to fire Malone yesterday."

Why I tell her this, I don't know. Is it because she is, despite the divorce, the most significant female in my life, and I am looking for comfort?

She responds softly, "I'm sorry. What happened, Randy?"

I start to say something cool, offhand—and stop. That's an old pattern, letting her know I'm hurting, and then dismissing any attempt she makes to sympathize. I answer, "It was a lot of things, building up. He's burned out. He made a bad mistake in writing orders. And then a girl he was treating, or trying to treat—well, she left AMA. And died a few hours later. I had to let him go."

"Is he getting any help?" she asks. "Any therapy?"

"I don't think so. I've told Allen about him, and Allen says he'd be willing to work with him. But he also says people burning out rarely acknowledge they need help until they're in the cinder stage."

A strange expression, a kind of bittersweet half smile, touches Sandra's lips, and then she starts down the steps with the girls. Something went awry there, something that made her decide not to talk to me any more. What was it?

At the bottom of the steps she hesitates and turns as if she is about to say something, then apparently thinks better of it and continues on her way. Vanessa calls out, "See you next Tuesday, Daddy," and Alexis lifts her hand in a gesture of farewell.

"Tuesday," I call, and then they turn the corner and are gone.

I put my hands in my pockets and start back toward Wilshire. I walk slowly to the stoplight on the corner, thinking about the separate pieces of my life. The father piece; the husband, no, ex-husband piece; the friend, the administrator, the doctor. They're like chess pieces, in a way. Their values change depending on what is expected of them as well as the stress placed on them. And shoring up one often seems to weaken another.

I wonder if that isn't what ages us more than the passing of years—the constant attempts to balance, to keep the pieces in a cogent pattern.

Ahead of me there is a restaurant that serves extraordinary omelettes. Am I hungry? Not really, but I should eat something before I go to the hospital.

When I enter the restaurant, it's still early for the dinner hour, just a little before 5:30; but the place is pretty well packed with celebrants from the festival. I put my name on the waiting list, and then go upstairs to sit at the small wine bar.

I don't drink alcohol in the twelve hours preceding a

shift, so I order Perrier with a lemon twist and sit there wishing it were a smoky glass of scotch. My mood is reflective and heading toward melancholy.

"It's part of living an examined life," Allen told me. "When you're trying to understand the mistakes you made in the past so you won't make them again, hindsight can be as enervating as the bends."

Probably if I weren't going on shift in a couple of hours, I'd be thinking about the hospital instead of the past. But since my shift is so imminent, my thoughts drift backward, and I find myself thinking about Lorna Elliott. Actually, she's been coming into my mind quite a bit during this whole escalating crisis with Malone.

There were two girls among the thirty-six students accepted into medical school the year I was. Lorna was one of them. She had, it seemed, everything going for her. She was attractive, brilliant; the youngest medical student in that class; and she consistently pulled down the highest marks.

I took her out on a date once and found it was an experience I didn't want to repeat. There was an intensity about her that was almost frightening. It was evident in class as well, but somehow what was acceptable in class was not acceptable in a one-to-one situation.

The first question I asked her was how she had come so far so fast. I really wanted to know, because it had taken me years to find the road I wanted to travel, and here was this dazzling young woman barely twenty who'd not only gotten everywhere before me but consistently bested me in all the exams.

"It's not all that complicated," she told me. "When I was quite young, I discovered a phenomenon about the human body that fascinated me. Fear produces adrenaline. Whatever you do while you're charged with adrenaline, you do much better and much faster than you would do otherwise. So I live my life as though I'm being chased by tigers. Which, for an ambitious woman in twentieth-century America, isn't a difficult fantasy to maintain."

But the intense patterning Lorna laid on her life couldn't tolerate failure. She didn't even take time to burn out. When a few of her grades started to slip, she panicked. The first time she got a C on an exam, she slashed her wrists and died.

At the class reunion I went to a couple of years ago, nobody wanted to talk about Lorna. Some people didn't even seem to remember she had existed. But she's one of the ghosts I carry around inside my head. She called me the night she committed suicide, but I was out.

The longer I sit there, the darker my thoughts become, and I'm grateful when I hear my name called. I follow the waiter to a corner table for two, wishing I were with a lovely, smiling woman who would distract me from my mood. I glance around the small dining room after I order my omelette. Everybody there seems to be in pairs.

The omelette, when it comes, is excellent, but I don't finish it.

When I leave the restaurant and walk the block and a half to my car, it is dusk. I glance into Hancock Park. There is no one there; the revelers are all gone. The booths and stages have been taken down, and on either side of the park, the museums are closed. It will soon be night.

NIGHT SHIFT

6:48 P.M.—As I enter the white corridor the events of the two days I have spent away from it seem remote, and I realize, perhaps consciously for the first time, that what I do here is what the philosophy professor from USC told me Western man rarely does: I inhabit the present moment.

I look around for Sy, who will be on shift with me until nine o'clock. I don't see him, but he could be in any one of the treatment rooms, or upstairs taking a dinner break.

I scan the on-call chart to see which doctors in the hospital proper are going to be available to me throughout the night, and note Jim Blandsford from pediatrics; a neurosurgeon and an orthopedic surgeon with whom I communicate well; a good ENT man. And Ahmad from cardiology. Oh well, four out of five's not bad.

I go into the doctors' room. Andy Donahue is there

waiting to tell me which patients he is leaving in my care.

Transfer of patient care during shift changeover time is one of the things I've worked hard on since becoming director at L.A. Memorial. When I was just starting out as an ER physician, putting in shift time at several hospitals, I remember there were times when the physician leaving communicated only minimal information to the physician coming on. And the notes tired ER doctors put on their charts as the end of their shift time approached were often so sparse, they were virtually useless.

So I've made it mandatory at L.A. Memorial that charting be as thorough at the end of a doctor's shift as it is at the beginning; and that the doctor going off shift wait until the doctor coming on has arrived so the two of them can discuss the most serious cases being transferred.

"What's hot?" I ask Andy.

"A kid with an ear I don't like the looks of," he replies, his long, scholarly face even more solemn than usual. "I've ordered a CBC. Then there's a guy who's hallucinating. His wife says she's been through it with him before, that it's an aftermath from exposure to dioxin in Vietnam. She says she can usually handle it, but that tonight she couldn't."

"What about the VA?" I ask.

"She told me they've seen her husband several times, but beyond prescribing tranquilizers there's nothing they can do. I think right now she just wants to be in a place where there are people around."

"Okay. What else?"

"A man with a bellyache who wants us to fix him fast so he can catch a ten P.M. flight to Cincinnati. Sy has a handle on the rest."

"Fine. Thanks, Andy." I nod and he is gone.

I am sitting at my desk going over the paperwork that

has accumulated when there is a light knuckle rap on the open door. I turn to see a slight, gray-haired man in a wrinkled business suit looking in at me.

"Dr. Sword?"

"Something I can do for you?"

He gives me a wan smile and hands me a white envelope. "By the powers vested in me by the Superior Court of the County of Los Angeles, I hereby serve this summons upon you. Sign here, please."

Wondering how he managed to infiltrate his way past the clerks who usually protect me from this kind of thing, I sign his damn form, and he leaves. I tear open the envelope, taking out the papers inside. They are from the law offices of Frank Gonzales and inform me that I am being sued by one Arturo A. Cabrillo; that if I wish to defend this lawsuit, I must, within thirty days, file a written response to the complaint. If I do not do so, my wages may be garnished and my property seized.

I note my first name is misspelled: "Randill."

The complaint is for personal injuries arising out of medical malpractice. I read through it quickly to get to the heart of the matter . . .

"That on or about September 27, 1981, plaintiff went to the premises of defendant's Los Angeles Memorial Medical Center for the purpose of receiving treatment of a cut sustained on the index finger of the right hand.

"That plaintiff believes that on or about September 27, 1981, at the premises of Los Angeles Memorial Medical Center the defendant failed to diagnose and properly treat him.

"The ligament of the plaintiff's right index finger had been severed and the defendant should have but failed to diagnose the cut ligament.

"That as a result of said negligent actions, plaintiff

continued to suffer great pain and lost the services of the finger of the right hand and has incurred additional medical expenses in attempts to get the hand repaired.

"WHEREFORE, plaintiff prays for relief as follows:

1. For general damages according to proof;
2. For medical expenses according to proof;
3. For costs of suit; and
4. For such further relief as the Court deems just and proper."

I close my eyes and lean back in my chair, searching for a face to match the name. Arturo Cabrillo . . . Arturo Cabrillo . . . I look at the summons again. When was he here? September 1981. That's years ago. It doesn't even say what day of the week it was, or what time of day.

How many patients have I seen in that span of time? With some quick mental calculations, I come up with a conservative figure of ten thousand.

Had Arturo Cabrillo died on a gurney in the trauma room in 1981, would I remember him? I doubt it. But a cut finger?

His chart, of course, can and will be retrieved and examined. The hospital attorneys my malpractice insurance pays for will delve into the case and most likely get it dismissed or settled for a nominal fee out of court. Sometimes they will make out-of-court settlements on totally fraudulent claims just to avoid the costs of a court hearing. But if I went to court and sat across from this man, would I even recognize him? I don't think so.

Yet now, through his attorney, Cabrillo has the power to state that he believes I failed to diagnose and properly treat him. And inevitably, I ask myself, did I? Did I see this man amid a crush of patients with more serious problems; and did I fail to look, to see enough?

I know I made some mistakes when I was starting out

in emergency medicine. While treating the victims of my first multiple-victim traffic accident, I left a hunk of glass the size of a quarter inside a deep cut I stitched up on a man's jaw. He came to see me a couple of months after the accident to show me the piece of glass he'd had removed. "I'm not going to sue you or anything," he said. "I just wanted to show you this so you'll be more careful from now on."

Careful.

For weeks after that, I'd wake up in the middle of the night not remembering the details of the bad dream that startled me into wakefulness, only that in it there was broken glass. I examined every wound I sutured from then on as though I were looking for the proverbial needle in hay.

Beginning to practice medicine is like beginning any other profession. What you know in theory needs experience to make it truly operable. By the time you finish your internship, you've read about every emergency procedure there is; you've assisted in performing a lot of them; and you've done many of them solo. You've also, you hope, mastered the art of convincing others you not only know how to perform every emergency procedure, you're an absolute whiz at it. Because in order to get hired after you've finished your internship, you have to portray confidence to the point of having a chip on your shoulder.

("Ever done an endotracheal intubation, Sword?" "Sure." "How about a subclavian?" "Hell, yes, a dozen of them.")

The procedures you're shaky on, you practice on cadavers after hours.

But no matter how confident you are, or pretend to be, the first time you find yourself in charge of a hospital emergency room, not knowing what's going to come through those swinging doors, you're scared. Every patient you see and treat successfully diminishes that fear. By the time you've seen hundreds, the fear has retreated into a dim corner of your psyche, but it doesn't ever go away.

And each time you're served a summons like this—it's happened to me half a dozen times at L.A. Memorial; it's happened to all the doctors on my staff, and none of them has yet been a legitimate case of malpractice—the fear stirs to life again.

I am holding the summons when Sy enters the doctors' room. He recognizes at once what I have in my hand. "Ah, a greeting from a friendly neighborhood barrister."

I nod.

"You know, I did a little statistical exercise once," he says. "Say the average ER doctor sees fifty-three hundred patients a year, and over the course of that year he is allowed one mistake—which he isn't, but we'll assume he is. That means he's expected to perform at a 99.998% efficiency level. I don't know. On my bad days, that seems a tad unrealistic."

I scribble "Get patient file on Arturo Cabrillo" and toss it in the out basket.

"So how has it been?" I ask, though I have a pretty good idea from the drawn look around his mouth.

He shrugs. "Dropped two. One car-crash victim. One gunshot wound in the head, which isn't too bad, I guess, for Mother's Day."

Mother's Day is street nomenclature for the day welfare checks are received.

Sy sits down on the chair next to mine and asks me what he came to ask: "How did it go with Malone?"

I haven't talked to Sy since I fired Malone. I was going to call him and tell him about it, but when I got home

Friday what I wanted most was to be distracted; so I ended up pacifying myself with TV sitcoms until I fell asleep.

I answer him now. "It was like . . . like . . . he was hanging onto something. But when I told him, he let go."

Sy nods. "It was probably hope." He gets up, starts for the door, hesitates. "Look, I think it may be a rough night. If you want me to stick around after nine, I will."

That's a generous offer, one I hope I don't have to accept. "Thanks."

After he leaves I go to the closet, take out a scrub suit, and put it on, wondering (not for the first time) who chose this particular grayish shade of green and why; it's not a cheerful color, nor, to me, even a soothing one. I put on the white coat over my scrubs and go out into the corridor.

Lily is the secretary on duty at the nurses' station. She's a black woman in her mid-thirties who's raising two daughters by herself. She tries to camouflage the fact that she is an attractive woman by drawing her hair back in a bun and wearing owlish glasses and baggy sweaters over her whites that conceal the outline of her rather remarkable bosom. In the eighteen months I've known her, she's gone from being mildly interested in to sharply militant about women's rights. For a while, she had most of the staff intimidated to the point where we wouldn't ask her to do things that we took for granted from Calvin Bixby.

I finally got fed up one day and confronted her.

"Shoot," she said, "you think I don't know that? One of the things we're learning at the woman's group I go to is to get all we can. I mean, *all*. And if we get more than our fair share, well, maybe it'll help balance the scales that have been out of whack so long."

Since that discussion, things have been more relaxed

between us. She'll ask me from time to time, "Dr. Sword, how come you don't have any women doctors on your staff? You think they're going to outshine you?"

"Tell you what, Lily," I reply. "You send me a good one and I'll put her as close to the top of my list as she belongs."

One reason I don't have any women EM physicians on my staff is because the turnover is so low here. I've only had occasion to hire two doctors since I became director, and in both instances, there weren't any female applicants. The entrance of women into emergency medicine is escalating, though. I'm going to have to hire a replacement for Malone, and perhaps I will have some women apply this time. I tell myself I wouldn't have any trouble working alongside a female EM physician. I think that's true.

I work well with the women doctors on the staff from upstairs. I have observed that their touch is softer than mine; the questions they ask are more subtle, even circuitous, yet they seem to elicit as much or more information than I do with my blunt, straightforward manner. They also remain extraordinarily calm in times of crisis. In fact, the worse things get, the calmer they seem to become.

There is something happening among women today, though, that mystifies me. There is something "joined" about them. I feel it when the women doctors walk into the board meetings together. I feel it among the women nurses. I notice it sometimes in stores when I witness an interaction between a woman customer and a woman clerk, and then, when the woman clerk turns to wait on me—it isn't there.

One day I asked Illana about it.

"Well, it's a kind of bonding," she said. "Members of any threatened minority have it, only usually they don't let it show, since that can be dangerous. But women are starting to get braver now."

Bonding. Knowing its name doesn't tell me what it is. I know it isn't the same thing as the friendship between Sy and me, because what we have has developed from our knowing each other for a long time and working together. But I see this bonding happen among women who don't even know each other.

Probably Lily is the one I should ask to explain it to me. When I feel brave enough. She came on at four today and she'll be here until midnight, when Calvin Bixby relieves her.

I ask her if the teleautograph is working. She replies that it is, but only the Lord Herself knows for how long.

The teleautograph is a machine designed to transmit test results from the hospital lab upstairs directly down to ER, thereby saving the ER secretary the necessity of spending time on the phone.

The only problem with it is, it works intermittently.

However, I'm always hopeful it will be working on Saturday nights when I want everything and everyone able to function at peak capacity.

As I stand next to Lily scanning the charts in the rack, she points to a shoebox on her desk. "My youngest made fudge today. You get hungry, just help yourself."

I lift up a corner of the lid and peek inside. The fudge is a dark, bittersweet color. A little after midnight is when the craving for chocolate usually hits me on the night shift, and then again before dawn. I also know how fast good things to eat can disappear around here, so I ask Lily, "Should you leave it out in plain sight like that?"

She smiles. "Nobody touches Lily's fudge without permission."

I leave the nurses' station carrying the chart of the child with the ear infection. Her name, I note, is Lac Wun Soo. She is four years old. When I enter the pediatrics room, her mother is standing next to the bed, holding her daughter's hand. The child's eyes are bright with fever; the last time it was charted it was 104 degrees. She is holding a kidney basin full of greenish yellow vomit. Both mother and daugher are silent, watching me carefully, though they quickly avert their gaze whenever I look directly at them.

Asian women are a mystery to me. They seem so fragile, and yet I know they're not. I am drawn by the blackness of their hair, their delicate bone structure, their soft voices.

"The Madame Butterfly syndrome. You just swallow all the culture clichés hook, line, and sinker, don't you, Sword?" Sy said to me once when I was waxing poetic about a Korean woman I had treated. "Listen. They are no more and no less exotic than any other females." But I am not convinced.

The child's eyes fasten on the silver otoscope I hold as I bend down to examine her ear. It hurts her to flex her neck, but she won't say so.

The tympanic membrane is red and bulging; there is no light reflex. At the very least it is acute purulent suppurative otitis media, inflammation of the inner ear. I hope that's all it is. But the child looks sicker than that. I won't know for certain until the results of the CBC Andy ordered come in.

I go back to the nurses' station, tell Lily to call Jim Blandsford and have him come down here stat, and then push the lab for the CBC results.

I scarcely have the words out before the teleautograph starts chattering. Lily and I exchange surprised glances. Seconds later, while she is on the phone to pediatrics, I am reading the child's CBC. Her white cell count is alarmingly high, over 20,000, confirming my suspicion that meningitis may be present. A spinal tap will have to be done as soon as possible, with parental consent.

Lily replaces the receiver and tells me Jim Blandsford is in a parent conference, but that word will be relayed to him to break it off and get down here.

I return to the examination room to inform the mother a specialist is on the way, and while I'm talking to her I notice, for the first time, an ugly bruise on her temple; there are several more on her right forearm. I ask her how it happened, but she shakes her head and murmurs, "Please pay attention only to my child."

Well, I think I know how it happened. The number of Asian women subjected to physical abuse from their husbands is higher than among blacks, Latins, or Caucasians.

For the thousands of Asians who have come to the United States the culture shock is overwhelming, and the males are venting their frustrations physically on their wives. Most of the women refuse to discuss their domestic crises. The ones who do make excuses for the husbands who beat them. "It is because he misses his home." "He cannot find work." "He is jealous of me because he has to take care of the children while I am away at work, and this demeans him."

No doubt all these things are true. But none of them are sufficient cause for one human being to inflict physical abuse on another. If I tell them this, they will look away from me, and their expressions become distant, unreachable.

Jim Blandsford walks into the room, moves to the child's side, and places his hand briefly over the mother's, who is still touching her daughter. He reads the CBC results I have entered on the chart and gently positions the child's head so that he can look into her ear.

Then he murmurs to me, "Transfer her upstairs." Placing an arm around the mother's shoulder, he guides her out of the room, explaining softly why her daughter must be admitted to pediatrics upstairs.

Luc Wun Soo's eyes follow her mother out into the corridor, but she doesn't cry; probably it hurts too much.

I am writing the transfer orders on her chart when Illana enters with two orderlies who wheel the gurney on which Lac Wun will be moved upstairs. Illana is brisk, efficient with the orderlies; incredibly gentle with the child—and as I leave the room she is smoothing the pillows and humming something that sounds like a Jamaican lullabye.

I pick up two more charts and enter the main treatment room. Roy Strickland, the man suffering from hallucinations, is lying quietly on bed 8; he appears to be sleeping.

Alfred is attaching EKG nodes to a patient of Sy's in an adjacent bed.

At the far end of the room I see Mr. Cowan, the man with the bellyache in bed 2. I decide to examine him first. He's a stout man in his early fifties with graying blond hair and a small paunch. I draw the curtain around his bed and ask him to tell me where it hurts.

"My right side, in from my hip bone," he tells me. "Look, Dr.—"

"Sword."

"—Dr. Sword, I don't know if the other doctor told you or not, but I've got a plane to catch at ten o'clock."

"He told me," I murmur, my fingers probing his abdomen.

He tries not to let me know I'm hurting him, but

when my fingers palpate the right lower quadrant, he flinches sharply. I do a rectal exam, and there is definite right-sided tenderness. There is also a positive psoas sign, pain on passive hyperextension of his thigh.

Illana joins me at his bedside. I write orders for a CBC and urinalysis on his chart and hand them to her, telling him I'll be back as soon as his lab tests are done.

"Doctor—"

I turn.

"I have to be on that plane. I'm meeting someone at midnight in Cincinnati."

"Perhaps you'd better make a phone call," I suggest.

"I can't do that. She's on a plane right now, flying in from Newark. Can't you just give me something for the pain and let me go?"

"Not until I know for certain what's wrong with you," I reply. "But I'll try and speed up your lab tests."

As I walk away, Illana is preparing the needle to draw his blood for the CBC, and I hear him say to her, "How can I make the doctor understand?"

"Understand what?" she asks.

But I don't wait to hear what it is I am supposed to understand.

Mr. Strickland is awake now and struggling to sit up. Alfred is taking his pulse and at the same time exerting gentle pressure on him to lie back down. I approach the bed and take my first close look at him. The man is thin and wasted-looking. His hair is dry, brittle, faded as if the color has somehow been bleached out of it. The shape of his head, the gaunt planes of his face have an almost skeletal aspect. I have seen that look in some of Jim Blandsford's cancer patients. It even has, I can't deny it, a certain ascetic beauty, like the faces of monks after periods of long fasting.

I scan his chart, noting he's a year younger than I am. I think back to what Andy Donahue told me of his history, and I am sharply aware—as I have been before when treating Vietnam veterans—of how close I came to participating in that war. If I had chosen to enter the Naval Air Corps instead of the Peace Corps, in all likelihood I would have been a combat pilot in Vietnam.

Roy Strickland was admitted into ER close to the end of Donahue's shift; Alfred was on the triage desk at the time (Eugene is there now), and so he must have been the one to admit him. No tests have been ordered. His pulse and blood pressure and temperature are all normal. He evidenced no sign of pain and offered no complaint when Andy initially examined him. However, at this moment, he scarcely seems to know where he is. "Mr. Strickland, how are you feeling?"

He doesn't respond or even glance at me. His eyes are as blank as the wall he's staring at.

I look at Alfred. There is something in his face I have seen before and have come to recognize. I live with the knowledge of Vietnam as a road I didn't take, but Alfred was *there*. Inevitably, certain patients open up memories of the time he spent as a combat nurse.

"Have you talked to his wife?" I ask.

He nods. "She's in the waiting room."

I motion Alfred outside to the corridor.

When we're standing there, I say, "Alfred, you know what's probably in store for us tonight?"

"Yeah," he murmurs softly.

"I know this man is ill," I say. "But it's not something we're equipped to deal with. Now I can release him, or I can bump him into the psych ward at County."

"I think you should talk to his wife," Alfred says with a stubborn note in his voice.

I hesitate. I don't want to talk to the man's wife because I don't think there's anything I can do for her husband. But I hear myself murmur "All right," and start down the corridor. I press the button that opens the doors into the waiting room. It's about half full, but I know at once which one is Mrs. Strickland.

She is sitting in a chair pulled away from the others, both hands around a Styrofoam cup half full of coffee. She's probably about Sandra's age. You can tell she was once a pretty woman, but her blonde hair is ragged; she is taut with stress; the jeans she is wearing are a couple of sizes too big; one of the straps on her sandals is broken.

I pull a chair next to hers and sit down.

She glances at me.

"Mrs. Strickland?"

"Yes."

"I'm Dr. Sword, the physician on duty now. I've just come from seeing your husband."

She nods.

"Can you tell me why you brought him in tonight?"

She looks down at the coffee cup she is holding, but doesn't answer right away. When she does, she spaces her words carefully. "Well, because there are times when I can't—I just can't be alone with him. He gets caught in some awful kind of time warp and thinks he's back in the war again."

After a moment, she continues, "He can't be left alone. Only he doesn't have anybody but me. So, I—I take him to emergency rooms. Different ones. I try not to go to the same one twice. Sometimes they let him spend the night, while I sit in the waiting room and try to get myself back together. Because eventually he comes out of it."

I am silent for a moment, wishing it were 3 A.M. on a week night so I wouldn't have to say this to her: "The

problem is, Mrs. Strickland, it's Saturday night. We don't
have a lot of empty bed space now, and later—"

"I know. Believe me, I know. I tried to tell myself,
Dorothy, it's Saturday night. They've got no room for Roy
on a Saturday night. But, you see, he was starting to get
bad, and I was falling apart."

"I can transfer him to County," I offer.

She shakes her head. "Being in a psych ward seems to
make him worse. All he needs is time."

Well, what can I say? What would Alfred have me
say?

While I'm trying to figure that out, she goes on. "I've
been sitting here thinking. Could you maybe just let him
stay in there until you need his bed? As soon as you do,
I'll take him somewhere else."

Perhaps I shouldn't grant her request, but how can I
refuse it? "I guess that'll be okay."

She nods and murmurs, "Thank you."

I start to get up, then sit down again. "Listen, there
has to be a better answer for you than this."

She shakes her head. "There isn't. I think back, sometimes, to the girl I was in high school, and the boy Roy
was. But there's nothing left of those two people now.
They just disappeared. The thing I don't understand is
how or why. I look around and I see people everywhere
whose lives are never touched by things like this—things
that have no answers."

I feel such an ache in the back of my throat, I can't sit
there with her any more. I head for the doors, punch
5-5-5-5, and go back into the white corridor.

8:20 P.M.—There are four new charts waiting in the chart
rack. As I draw near the nurses' station Lily is pointing at

the teleautograph, which is chattering efficiently, transmitting the results of Mr. Cowan's CBC and urinalysis. I'm not surprised to see the results: leukocytosis. It completes the classic symptomatology of appendicitis. I ask Lily to call upstairs for a surgical admit, and then go to tell Mr. Cowan he won't be catching that plane.

"The hell I won't," is his fast response.

Illana has accompanied me to fill out the admit forms.

"Mr. Cowan—" she begins.

I cut her off without meaning to. "Look, maybe you didn't understand what I said. You need to have that appendix removed *now*."

"I'll have it done in Cincinnati," he replies. "After—" he stops.

"After what?" I ask.

But he doesn't reply.

"We can get word to her, Mr. Cowan," Illana says softly.

He shakes his head. "No. I have to be there."

I have no idea what they're talking about, but I think whatever it is can't be as important as making him understand the seriousness of his condition.

"Listen," I say, "if you don't have that appendix out you're running the risk of perforation, peritonitis, and appendiceal abscesses, any one of which can be fatal."

"It's going to have to wait a few hours," he says. "Now, can you give me something for the pain?"

"Not a damn thing," I respond angrily.

"Dr. Sword, may I speak to you for a moment?" Illana's voice is urgent.

I look up at her. I'm so angry at Cowan I almost forgot she was there.

I follow her out into the corridor.

"I think you should know why he feels he has to catch that plane."

"Go on."

"He has a daughter he's never seen. The girl's been trying to trace him for three years, and two months ago, when she found him, they arranged this meeting. There is no way he's not going to be on that plane for Cincinnati tonight."

"Illana, you know what the risks are with a bad appendix."

She nods. "But from his point of view, this may be the most important event of his life."

I am still holding the man's chart and still angry, too. However, I scrawl orders on it for an antibiotic, which will, I hope, diminish the developing infection, and then I go back to talk to him.

"Look," I say, "once you're on that plane, I want you to assume what is known as Fowler's position. Sit with your back up at least forty-five degrees from horizontal, and put a blanket roll under your knees so you're not stretching your abdominal muscles. Should your appendix perforate —which I hope to God it doesn't—pus will settle by gravity into the lowest part of your abdomen, so there will be a better chance for an abscess to form and wall off the infection. And from this moment on, don't eat or drink anything. When you get to Cincinnati, kiss your daughter and then head for the nearest emergency room."

He nods, giving me a grateful look, but I am still tempted to pop him on the jaw and send him up to surgery comatose. The bottom line is, I have to protect myself and the hospital. I say, "You're going to have to sign an AMA form."

"What's that?" he asks, wincing with pain as he reaches for the paper bag containing his clothes.

"A statement that you are leaving this hospital against medical advice."

"I'll sign it."

Illana's waiting in the corridor, and I tell her to get the form, remembering glumly Malone's AMA patient, the girl who died.

Then I head for the chart rack again. I am reading the top one when Lily says softly, "Dr. Sword—" She is pointing down the corridor. Roy Strickland is standing there. "Should I call—" her voice trails off. She was going to say "security," but there is no need.

Roy is wearing the standard hospital gown, knee-length, open down the back. His arms and legs are as thin as pickets. He moves toward the waiting-room doors, hesitates; turns, starts toward us, hesitates again.

I have seen people lost before, like Roy. Early in my career, I worked weekends in the psychiatric ward at New Mexico State Mental Hospital, providing emergency care to mentally disabled patients. They were so disconnected, those people. I could treat their cuts and illnesses, minister to their bodies. But the painful places their minds inhabited were inaccessible to me. I'll never forget the feeling of release I felt when I walked out of that hospital on Monday mornings.

I move now quickly, silently toward Roy. He's staring right at me, but I know he doesn't see me. As I draw near, Alfred comes out of the main treatment room and puts an arm around Roy's shoulders.

Roy leans against him, head going down. His breathing is audible, sounding dry and strained as Alfred leads him back to bed, saying softly, "You need to sleep, Roy. I know it's noisy in here, but if you rest awhile, you can go home."

Roy moves his head, and though I can't tell what the gesture means, I know he's heard Alfred.

"Doctor?"

It's Lily summoning me from the other end of the corridor. "Telephone. It's Mrs. Malone."

I tell her I'll take the call in the doctors' room.

8:57 P.M.—Since Friday afternoon, I've been feeling uneasy about Malone and trying to ignore the feeling, or rationalize it, or push it into a corner of my mind where I won't have to acknowledge it. But now that I have to speak to Jill, it all comes back.

I pick up the phone. "This is Randall Sword."

"Dr. Sword, I'm sorry to bother you—but I wonder if you've seen Michael, or if he's been at the hospital."

Her voice is anxious, close to tears.

"I haven't seen him," I reply.

She is silent and I ask her simply, "Jill, how is he?"

"Well, he's—I don't know. He won't talk to me. But he hasn't slept at all since, well, for two nights. When he left the house today I ran after him and asked him where he was going, and he said he wanted to pick up some of his things at the hospital."

"What time was this?"

"Around three this afternoon."

I glance up at the clock, picturing her sitting in that small apartment for over five hours.

"Look," I say, "I'm sure he'll come home soon. But if he should happen to show up here, I'll have him call you, I promise."

She murmurs a soft "Thank you" and hangs up.

I sit there staring at the phone. Damn it, I worried about Malone while he was here and now I'm worrying about him when he isn't. I'm concerned about Jill, too.

But as it turns out, I don't stay focused on either one very long because Sy sticks his head in the door to tell me, "Central Dispatch is on the biocom, Randy. A repair crew was working on a storage tank that was supposedly emptied of liquefied gas this morning, and it collapsed in on them. Ten men inside. They're getting them out now. They want to know how many criticals and how many minors we can take."

Jesus. I'm on my feet at once, out in the corridor, counting beds, assessing our capability.

Both beds are available in the trauma room.

Roy Strickland is in the main treatment room, and two of Sy's patients. That leaves two empty beds there with monitoring facilities. Three if I need them, because I can and will move Roy.

Sy and I are free. I can count on the in-house doctor from upstairs; more, if I call a Code Yellow, which is our disaster alert.

But there's only one operating-room crew working at night.

I can call the nursing supervisor and ask her to bring in another one if things get bad enough—but there are problems involved in doing that. For one thing, once they're contacted, it can take the members of the second OR crew as long as an hour to assemble at the hospital. And for another, the hospital administration frowns sharply on the costs involved.

So all I can really do now is make an educated guess. If we accept three criticals, we can send one straight up to OR and hope we can keep the other two stabilized while waiting their turn. If my guess is wrong, well, I'll just have to call the nursing supervisor and try to persuade her to bring in another OR crew.

I say to Sy, "Tell them we can take three criticals, two minors . . . if there are any minors."

As Sy talks to the dispatcher on the biocom, Eugene enters the corridor from the waiting-room end, hurrying into the trauma room to help Illana check the crash carts. Until we get through this, there will be no one at the triage desk.

At the nurses' station, Lily is busy on the phone, alerting the hospital proper: OR, the surgery crew, the on-call physicians, the lab technicians, trying to get us a second x-ray technician, the portable x-ray machine, an inhalation therapist.

I swiftly scan the charts in the rack, assessing our backup (the patients waiting to be seen), paying no attention to names or ages, only to symptoms. There is a scalp laceration in suturing; a child with a sore throat in the pediatrics room; an asthma attack in ENT; a rash of unexplained origin in the general treatment room; an eighteen-year-old girl in ob/gyn who may be miscarrying. A patient Sy has assessed is in x-ray getting a skull series. I can move any or all of these patients back out into the corridor or the waiting room if I have to.

Every emergency room in the area will be involved in accepting the victims, so we may not even get the three I've said we can take. But we could be simultaneously hit with other trauma victims—gunshot wounds, stabbings, car-accident victims. Multiple-victim car crashes are more frequent after nine o'clock on a Saturday night than at any other time.

Should all our staff be working at capacity, Lily will inform Central Dispatching that Los Angeles Memorial is closed to ambulances only, meaning we can accept only walk-ins.

But there have been nights when all the hospitals in

the area have called into Central Dispatching that they were closed. Then, of course, everybody is automatically open again, and as Calvin Bixby puts it, the real game of Russian roulette begins.

9:17 P.M.—I wait beside the biocom for the rescue ambulance drivers to call and give me their assessment of the victims they are bringing in.

Even though I know how futile it is, I find myself trying to anticipate what the injuries might be. If the tank collapsed because of leaking gas exploding inside it, we could be presented with respiratory failures. Barring that, we're going to be dealing with injuries presented by the collapse of the structure itself—internal injuries, crush injuries, lacerated, possibly severed limbs . . .

And then, of course, there is the ER version of Murphy's Law. Given a disastrous situation, if something worse can happen, it will. People on the verge of strokes or heart attacks can be catapulted into such episodes by trauma to other parts of their bodies or simply by the stress of being in the midst of a catastrophe.

Every time an EM physician thinks he's seen it all, life one-ups him.

The hardest thing for me, when coping with multiple-victim episodes, is not to get too deeply involved with one patient. My job is to treat them in order of the seriousness of their injuries, stabilize each one as quickly as I can, and move on to the next one.

The worst moments in my role as an ER physician have been when two patients with life-threatening injuries have been brought in within seconds of each other.

One Labor Day weekend, an RA brought in a man who had been shot in the head, just as a police unit brought in a scoop-and-run car-accident victim. Since the second victim had not gone through Central Dispatch, no attempt had been made to assess our capability. Both victims were young men in their twenties; both were extremely critical; both needed help immediately.

I made my decision on the basis that the gunshot wound was probably fatal . . . and I simply let him go while I stabilized the car-accident victim. Later, the neurosurgeon from upstairs assured me the man with the gunshot wound was beyond treatment. But those words haunt me. Probably fatal.

I am grateful now that Sy is here. It tilts the odds a little in our favor.

I grow conscious of my own breathing and heartbeat as I wait for the call from the RAs. Once I am involved with multiple-trauma patients, the thing that keeps me going is the adrenaline-produced high Lorna Elliott wanted to live off. But you can't live off it. You save it for moments like this.

9:24 P.M.—The biocom crackles into life. "This is City Rescue Two, come in Memorial. Can you hear us?"

"This is L.A. Memorial Hospital base station. I can hear you loud and clear."

"We are enroute with two victims. The first is an approximately thirty-five-year-old male who was initially unconscious but now is coming around. His BP is ninety over zero and he has a weak pulse of one-twenty with the MAST suit inflated. He has a large hematoma on the left side of his skull; seems to hurt all over, but is moving all extremities."

"How is his breathing?"

"He's anxious and breathing at twenty or so, but exchanging air well."

"Pupils?"

"Equal and reactive to light."

"Okay, we'll be ready for him. What about the second one?"

"Victim number two is a twenty-six-year-old male; he is conscious and lucid. Complains of pain in his neck and shoulder and left leg, and tingling in his hands. We have immobilized the neck with a cervical collar; he's on a backboard, and we've put an air splint on the left leg."

"Do you have vital signs?"

"BP one-forty over seventy-five; pulse one-ten; respirations at eighteen. Our ETA is now six minutes."

"Ten-four, Rescue Two. This is L.A. Memorial clearing the frequency."

I stand next to the biocom, trying inside my head to visualize the injuries.

Although the first victim sounds the most critical and that is the way the RA attendants have assessed it, he may not be.

The first man seems to have had a concussion, and is coming around, but is in shock. Could be internal bleeding or a crushed pelvis.

The neck injury of the second victim could involve a spinal injury.

I've been through this so many times. Until they get here, it's like playing some weird game of Blindman's Bluff.

I decide I will assess the first victim right here in the corridor and have Sy take the neck and leg injury in the main treatment room, thereby leaving one trauma bed still open.

Just as the red lights of the RA unit flash against the mesh-covered panels at the emergency entrance, the in-house doctor, Phil Mayer, enters the corridor from the waiting room.

"How many are you getting?" he asks, coming to stand beside me.

I shake my head. I don't know.

"OR's in use," he says. "They started an operation just before they got the alert."

"How long will they be?"

"I didn't ask."

Well, I can't worry about that now.

Sy comes out of the main treatment room as the doors fly open and victims one and two are wheeled in.

The man with the head injury on the first gurney is in shock. His face in the fluorescent light is bone white. His skin is moist, cool. His neck veins are flat. His breathing is rapid, shallow, but without difficulty. He needs immediate fluid replacement; at first saline solutions, then blood if the BP is not raised in a few minutes.

I sure as hell can't treat him in the corridor.

"Want me to take him?" Phil asks.

I nod yes, pointing toward the main treatment room, wanting still to keep a bed open in the trauma room if I can. We told Central Dispatch we could take three, and three is probably what we'll get.

Sy helps wheel the second victim with the possible spinal injury into the trauma room, and I hear him asking the patient rapid-fire questions in a loud voice:

"Tell me what happened."

"Something heavy fell on me."

"Where did it hit you?"

"I don't know. Everywhere. It was like being in a—in

a metal tent that collapsed, you know? Just suddenly, wham."

"Did anything hit your head?"

"I don't know. No."

"Did you pass out?"

"I don't think so."

"What hurts most?"

"My leg."

"Does it hurt to breathe?"

"Jesus, everything hurts."

"Take a deep breath. Does that hurt?"

"No."

"Any pain in your belly?"

"No."

"Back?"

"No."

"Any tingling in your fingers?"

"Yes."

While the patient is struggling to answer Sy's questions, Eugene and the orderly assisting are inserting IV lines, a catheter, drawing blood samples. This is why Sy's voice is so loud. He has to hold onto the man's full attention despite all the things that are being done to him.

"Do you have heart trouble?"

"No."

"Any problems with your kidneys?"

"No."

"Any allergies?"

"No."

"How many fingers am I holding up?"

"Three."

Then Lily's voice cuts through Sy's. "Dr. Sword! Biocom!"

I am there in one thin second.

"This is City Rescue Five. Can you hear us, L.A. Memorial?" The voice at the other end of the biocom sounds young, and panicked.

"This is L.A. Memorial. I hear you."

"We have an approximately forty-year-old man sweating heavily; poor color. His vital signs are blood pressure two-ten over one-twenty; pulse one-forty; respirations twenty-four and shallow. The firemen said when they pulled him out he had a five-hundred pound hunk of steel on his chest. Our ETA is four minutes."

I responded tightly, "Make it faster if you can, Rescue Five."

I don't have to try and second-guess this one, it's a flail chest, one of the ER physician's nightmare injuries. A flail chest occurs when the integrity of the rib cage is broken and when the victim breathes in, or tries to, the chest goes in instead of out. Each breath the victim tries to take diminishes the oxygen supply, thereby creating a vacuum until no air at all is being exchanged and the person is literally suffocating.

I am watching the clock.

"Call Central Dispatching and tell them we're closed to any more criticals," I murmur to Lily.

She shakes her head. "Everybody is closed."

The hell with it.

I focus on the sound of a rising siren, coming closer. I hope it's Rescue 5.

Eugene is assisting Sy. Illana is with Phil Mayer. Alfred will be assisting me. He comes to wait beside me, and we're standing by the double doors when the mesh panels turn red.

The eyes of the victim on the gurney that is wheeled through the door are terrified. He's not getting any air.

I run beside the gurney helping to wheel it into the trauma room; then I help transfer the patient to the Stryker bed and ask for and have an endotracheal tube placed in my waiting hand.

I position the tube in space above the terrified eyes, praying that I place it at precisely that point where the trachea divides into the right and left main stems. First I lay him on his back, tilt his head backward into the "sniffing position," force his jaw open. I can't see anything but blood.

"Give me some suction!"

The patient is struggling desperately for air, feet moving, arms trying to reach up and keep the six-inch-long curved blade with a light on the end from going down his throat.

"Tie down his arms and legs. We have to keep him still."

Alfred quickly places restraints over both ankles and wrists.

The man's chest heaves in labored efforts at respiration. He is sweating; his left chest is sucked in several inches as he fights against us. His color becomes ashen.

I murmur to Alfred, "Do your best to hold his head still or I'll never get this tube down him."

The man succeeds in twisting his head from side to side no matter how hard Alfred tries to hold him. Between the blood being coughed up and the tongue pushing out my blade, I can't get the tube in.

Sweat is running off my face. I am getting nowhere. A queasy feeling churns my stomach. I have two choices: I can do a tracheostomy (cut a hole in his trachea just below the Adam's apple and stick the endotracheal tube down the hole). Or I can paralyze him with Anectine (succinylcholine). Anectine is a skeletal muscle relaxant derived from the curare plant. Amazon jungle tribesmen tip their hunting spears with it to bring down large animals. Its effects are startling, sometimes even terrifying. The patient given Anectine becomes, literally, too relaxed to breathe. I administered it once to a patient who was as panicked as this man is so I could intubate him. When I put the endotracheal tube into his throat, I encountered a large tumor which blocked the insertion of the tube. Well, I knew if I couldn't get the tube in, I'd lose him right then and there, because his own ability to inhale and exhale had been rendered useless by the Anectine, so I worked the tube and worked it until it finally slid past the tumor.

I say to Alfred, "We'll have to go with Anectine. Give him forty milligrams IV. But load him up with Valium first."

Alfred moves quickly, following my orders.

After the Anectine is given IV, there is a tense period of thirty to sixty seconds before the drug takes effect. The first sign is fasciculation, small involuntary contractions, of the muscles. Then, suddenly, nothing. The arms, legs, head stop moving; breathing stops; not even the eyelids flutter. But the man can feel, hear, see everything.

The effect lasts several minutes, and it is during this time I can intubate him and hook him up to a breathing machine.

Once the tube is in, I release the breath I didn't even know I was holding.

"Positive pressure," I tell the inhalation therapist, but there is no need. The therapist is adjusting his dials; the flow of life-giving air is entering the man's lungs. Already his eyes are less terrified.

I ask for an x-ray to check the placement of the tube, then go back into the corridor to the nurses' station.

"You can relax," Lily tells me. "Central Dispatch called. We're not getting any more. At least not from the tank collapse."

I nod, feeling, then, all the things you eventually experience in the aftermath of one of these episodes—exhaustion, relief, the ebbing of your own fear—and I say to Lily, "Let's set up the charts."

When we're hit with a multiple-victim disaster like this, the victims have no names, no identities; they exist for us only by the nature of their injuries. So right now, all I have to identify them in my head is "Shock," "Spinal," and "Flail Chest."

But once everything is being done for them that can be done, Lily begins to put their charts together, writing down their names, dates of birth, addresses, places of employment, whether or not they have insurance, and so on. And then they begin to assume identities.

I walk with Lily back into the trauma room. My Flail Chest cannot talk, but Alfred has placed his wallet on the countertop. His name is Daniel Martin. He's forty-two years old. Folded around a borrower's card from the Alhambra Public Library is a notice for an overdue book.

Sy's patient is voluble in his response to Lily's questions. He tells us his name is Peter Gluck; he's twenty-six; he has a three-month-old baby daughter named Melinda. His wife's name is Jessie. He wants to know if his wife has been called; how long he's going to be laid off work; whether he will get disability. All the questions of a survivor.

Across the hall in the main treatment room, Phil's patient has come out of shock and murmurs responses to Lily's questions in an agitated, fearful voice. His name is Jeffrey Nolan; he's only nineteen, and he doesn't yet really comprehend what's happened to him.

"I think he has internal abdominal injuries," Phil tells me. "Could be a ruptured spleen. X-rays haven't come back yet. But he's going to need an exploratory, and the sooner the better."

"That makes three," I say. "I've got a broken rib cage that needs stabilizing; and Sy's patient, at the least, has a fractured shoulder and tibia. Think we can get them to bring in another OR crew?"

He shrugs. "We'll take turns trying. Between the two of us, maybe we can wear them down. Do you want to make the first call, or shall I?"

"You," I say without hesitation.

Lily sticks her head in the door. "We got some relatives out in the waiting room wanting to know how these three gentlemen are doing."

I tell Eugene to go out and inform the men's relatives they are, ultimately, all going to be okay—Eugene is wonderful at being the bearer of good news—and then I follow Lily back out to the nurses' station.

"Well, we got through that one," I say.

"Sure," she says, "don't we always. Here, have yourself a piece of fudge."

I surprise myself by refusing. Usually when I've come through a catastrophe I want chocolate and my staff knows it, only I don't feel that way right now. Well, maybe it's just the burden of the backup. I have three surgical admits, patients needing to be seen in every treatment room, and more people out in the waiting room.

And in the back of my mind, there's the gnawing worry about Malone.

Sy joins me at the chart rack. "I'll stick around awhile longer to help you wade through this batch at least."

I'm grateful as hell, but I wonder if he's doing it because he's feeling what I am—that there's still something out there waiting to happen.

In the hours up to midnight, the treatment rooms are cleared out, filled up, cleared out again.

We're so busy, I ask Illana to do some suturing. She took the course recently, and she's competent.

We get two gunshot wounds, but neither of them is serious: a poker player shot in the thigh by a loser at his table; an aspiring fourteen-year-old burglar peppered in the leg with shotgun pellets as he was running away from the irate woman whose house he broke into.

The policeman guarding the young burglar starts to help himself to Lily's fudge.

"Didn't your momma ever tell you you shouldn't take things that don't belong to you?" she demands. "That's stealing."

The cop, a grizzled veteran, almost drops the fudge, then replaces it carefully in the box.

Lily leaves at 12:00 as Calvin Bixby takes over.

A few minutes later, Sy, in street clothes, yawns. "Good night," he says. "I'll be hibernating until April."

I watch him walk down the corridor. He's been on duty seventeen hours and his movements show it.

I owe him one.

1:37 A.M.—I step outside the doors at the ambulance entrance, needing to breathe air that isn't permeated with the smell of blood, sweat, and urine.

In the hour and a half since Sy left, I have . . .

—Extracted from a sixteen-year-old girl's vaginal vault a tampon that looked as if it had been rammed in with a pile driver.

—Sutured a deep cut on a dishwasher's index finger, finding myself momentarily cheered by the man's smile when Ramon translated my instructions that he should not immerse his hands in water for a week.

—Denied a woman's request for diet pills after she informed me tearfully that she had gained two pounds since eight o'clock that morning.

—Called the nursing supervisor upstairs to reinforce Phil's plea to bring in another OR crew, and was told, "Your concern for your patients is appreciated, Randy, but the staff we've got will simply have to work double time. We've been through this kind of thing before, and as you know, the administration always feels it's best to be conservative."

—Treated a pizza delivery man who was stabbed in the arm with an ice pick by a customer who had ordered Canadian bacon on his pizza and got pepperoni instead.

—Removed two wadded-up $100 bills from the anus of a woman who, after being robbed twice last month, was determined nobody was going to get her money this month. The only problem was, she herself couldn't retrieve the money. I wasn't able to feel it either when I examined her, so I was skeptical about her story. But I ordered x-rays, and when I placed them on the light screen there was the money, about as far up as it could go. I prescribed suppositories so she could expel it.

—Watched Eugene cure a six-foot-three longshoreman's chronic hiccups by brandishing an eight-inch hypodermic needle, assuring the man his hiccups would surrender to the injection he was about to administer. Before the needle grazed the man's skin, the hiccups died mid-larynx.

Eugene is proud of the skill he has developed using that needle with hiccup cases, and I am proud, too, that I have succeeded in convincing Eugene that a prolonged case of hiccups can indeed qualify as a medical emergency.

Early in my career as an ER physician, I learned that although members of the emergency-medicine profession generally agree about what the function of an emergency room should be, they do not agree about what constitutes an emergency. And so I have instructed my staff to operate under one simple rule: Until the patient can be seen by a physician, it is the patient who defines the emergency.

Eugene has been slower to come around to this way of thinking than anybody else, and I'm always uneasy when he is on the triage desk for fear he will turn away someone who really needs help.

Standing now beneath the red-and-white illuminated EMERGENCY sign, breathing in the night air, absorbing the silence, I try to replenish my energy.

Unfortunately, the sense of uneasiness that has been haunting me since Friday will not go away, and suddenly I am remembering nights in Ethiopia when I went to watch the Hyena-man of Harar.

For the sake of coins tossed to him by tourists—and also, I think, simply because he enjoyed doing it—the old man would scavenge a gunny sack full of meat scraps from restaurants and take it to the outskirts of Addis Abbaba at night to feed the hyenas. He would kindle a small fire and the hyenas would gather in the darkness beyond it. You could see pairs of eyes, yellow and glittering. At first the old man would toss the meat out to where the hyenas waited. Then, slowly, by throwing the meat scraps closer and closer to the fire, he would see how close he could get the animals to come.

The animals seemed sinister to me, much more so than lions. I knew their jaws were strong enough to crush an elephant's thigh bone in seconds. My students told me many stories about how intelligent they were. But then, I thought, scavengers always are intelligent. I used to wonder what if, some night when the meat is gone, they don't fade back into the darkness, but keep coming closer.

Good God, why am I thinking about them now and feeling somehow threatened?

1:43 A.M.—I go back inside.

Daniel Martin, the man with the flail chest, is in surgery.

Jeffrey Nolan, whom Phil treated for shock, has been admitted upstairs and is in preop.

Peter Gluck is still in the trauma room, and his wife has come back to sit with him.

Attached to the top of one of two charts that have been placed in the rack during my respite I see an index card that says in large block letters:

G-U-E-S-S W-H-O'S H-E-R-E

As I approach the nurses' station, Calvin Bixby glances up. "I'll give you a clue if you need one."

I nod. "Go ahead."

"Crown of thorns."

"Harold," I say.

"Okay, hotshot, next time no clues."

I pick up the chart.

Harold is one of our perennials. He comes in, on the average, once every other month, usually after midnight, and usually during the first three days of the month.

He's a twenty-seven-year-old black man who looks fifty because life has cast him in an unchanging role: victim.

When he was seven years old, he was standing in line waiting to buy a popsicle from the Good Humor man when the hand brake on the ice cream truck failed and the vehicle rolled backward, knocking Harold down and crushing his legs. As he puts it, "Not a year of my life has gone by since that time, doc, when I haven't been hit by something."

His body testifies to that fact. He has suture scars on his chest, abdomen, neck, and back, and of course the massive scarring from the open reductions performed on his legs. His appendix and gall bladder have been taken out, and one kidney.

He has become an expert in litigation from appearing in court so many times to seek recompense for the malevolent events that mysteriously continue to plague him.

He is as skinny as the edge of a door, yet from the accounts given by his various lovers who sometimes accompany him to the emergency room, he eats like a horse.

The last time I had Harold admitted up into the hospital—for acute pancreatitis—and they were transferring him from the gurney to a hospital bed, something ("It has to be my aura, don't you think, doc?") caused the bed to collapse. Harold crashed to the floor and suffered a whiplash injury, and the hospital's lawyers breathed a collective sigh of relief when he accepted a reasonable out-of-court settlement. "You folks been taking care of me for years," he explained. "No way am I going to stick it to you."

I pick up his chart. Under presenting symptoms, Illana has written simply "Stomach pain." He's been put in the main treatment room, two beds down from Roy.

Harold is lying still when I draw near. His eyes are closed. His face has—I've noticed it before—an incredible sweetness to it.

When he opens his eyes, I can see he really is in pain.

"What is it this time, Harold?"

"I don't know, Dr. Sword. I just can't seem to keep

nothing on my stomach. And it hurts something fierce."

Well, I think I might know what it is.

Harold has been drinking heavily during the past couple of years, and his liver is beginning to act up. I've remonstrated with him about his increasing alcohol consumption, but he just smiles at me and says, "Sometimes things get so dark, you got to get your own glow on."

He'll have to have a series of lab tests. I tell him that.

He nods. "Is Alfred on tonight? Last time I was in, he and I had a real good talk about black holes and white dwarfs. You know anything about such things, Dr. Sword?"

"Not much," I reply. Nor am I in a mood, tonight, to discuss astronomy. Harold perceives this, gives me a sympathetic glance, and is silent.

He is an acutely intuitive man. I suspect he has learned how not to trespass on other people's boundaries because he has had to guard his own so carefully. He is black, homosexual, and a victim. The fact that he has survived at all bears testimony to his skill at negotiating his way through all kinds of enemy territory.

I write the orders on Harold's chart for liver function tests; leave him; pick up the second chart in the rack and go back into the main treatment room to examine a Mr. Richard Mudge, whose complaint is insomnia.

Although we see a fair number of people during the early-morning hours who come in because they can't sleep, Eugene finds this complaint ridiculous. I've explained to him that most of the patients who define their sleeplessness as an emergency only do so after they've spent four or five nights tossing and turning, but he still has trouble accepting it. So I wonder how Mr. Mudge got past him at the triage desk.

He is an intense-looking thirty-two-year-old man with prominent ears. The circles under his eyes are as dark as

hickory ash. He has cranked the bed into a sitting-up position and gives me an appraising glance as I draw the
curtain.

Before I can ask him anything, he says, "The only
reason I'm here is because I haven't figured out the logic to
this. Now, I should be able to sleep. Since I can't, there
must be a logical reason why."

Well, I think one reason he can't sleep is because
physically he's coiled himself around his problem like a
taut spring. Tension is evident in every muscle of his body.
I say, hoping to relax him a little, "You know, sometimes
people doze off, and don't remember sleeping. They think
they've been awake all night, but they really haven't."

The look he gives me is disparaging. "I know exactly
how long I've been awake. Seventy-five hours and fourteen
minutes."

"I see. Has this ever happened to you before?"

"Twice. The first time was when I was seven years
old. My dog was going to have puppies, and I didn't want
to miss it. And then again when I was twenty-three. I had
decided to propose marriage to an older woman, and I
couldn't sleep until I'd done it. After I did it, I slept for a
week."

I'm curious as hell to know whether the woman said
yes or no, but I can't ask him that.

"This time," he continues, "there is no reason. I have
been probing the parameters of my life for three days, and
there is no reason."

"What sort of work do you do?" I ask.

"I design chips."

"Chips?"

"Computer chips. No problem there. My last one was
a horse-race handicapper. It does exactly what it was designed to do."

"You mean it picks winners?"

"On a muddy track in Tiajuana, yes."

"I see. Well, have you moved recently? Sometimes a—"

"No. I own my house. I have lived in it for seven years. I am not contemplating moving. I doubt I will ever move. I have not purchased a new bed nor rearranged my furniture. My sex life is adequate for my needs. Nobody I care about has died. There is, you see, no logic to it. That's why I'm here. I want you to tell me what's wrong."

"Well, I—"

"Of course I know my circuit design is complex. You can't zero in on what's wrong with me like you can on a computer. So I'd like my blood checked and my urine; a complete set of x-rays; also any diagnostic test you can think of to elicit the cause of my sleeplessness. I have insurance that will pay for whatever it costs."

I hesitate. Except for the ashen circles under his eyes, Richard seems to be in excellent health. He has a runner's heartbeat of forty-eight beats per minute. His temperature and blood pressure are normal.

He frowns at my hesitation. "There is a widely accepted theory among sleep researchers you may not be aware of, doctor. Human beings require a certain amount of dream time, which is provided to them during their normal sleep pattern. If they are deprived of that, other imbalances follow. So, I think it's perfectly logical for you to do as I ask."

I scrawl orders for a CBC, glucose, a set of electrolytes, BUN (blood urea nitrogen), and urinalysis on his chart. But I'm not going to hurry the lab on these. Maybe while he's waiting for his test results, he'll fall asleep.

2:07 A.M.—Mr. Gluck is wheeled out of the trauma room and taken upstairs to preop, which should make me feel better, but it doesn't.

I go to check on Roy Strickland, who is lying quietly, his eyes focused, as nearly as I can tell, on a tiny hairline crack in the ceiling.

I go back out into the corridor. It's quiet now; too quiet, I think. I wonder how Mrs. Strickland is doing.

I'm starting down the corridor toward the waiting room to find out, when suddenly the doors open and a white-haired gentleman wearing a cape, tuxedo, and top hat strides toward me.

Big Tim is right on his heels.

"Goddamn if he didn't figure out the code," Tim tells me. "He's been sitting out there for a couple of hours, and I thought he was waiting for somebody. Then he up and opens the door."

This is the first time that I know of that somebody dressed in a tuxedo has been in the white corridor. It's also the first time any nonstaff person has used the code to open those doors. And although sitting in the waiting room, watching staff members punch 5-5-5-5 to open the doors, and then doing it yourself doesn't constitute an intellectual feat, it does take more than an average amount of chutzpah. I regard the old man with interest.

"Who's in charge here?" he demands.

Calvin Bixby grins and points at me.

"Is that true, young man?"

It's been a while since anybody has addressed me that way.

I nod.

"Where is your phone? I want to place a call to the White House."

"The White House?" I echo, feeling foolish, wondering if he's a congressman or a senator.

"You have a special phone to the White House. I want to use it."

I think I'm beginning to understand.

When the president is visiting Los Angeles, several twenty-four-hour emergency rooms in the area are equipped with a special phone in case of an emergency medical situation involving the president. How this old gentleman found out about the phones, I have no idea.

"We have no telephone line to the White House per se," I explain. "It's a line to the president's personal physician."

"I know. That's who I want to talk to."

"Well, but you see, that phone is only operable when the president is in town."

The old man looks at me sharply. I can tell he's wondering whether I'm lying. I'm glad I'm not.

"I've discovered an elixir, young man, and I want the president to have it."

"An elixir?"

He frowns impatiently. "Is there someone with more authority I can speak to?"

I'm tempted to point to Calvin Bixby, but I don't.

"I'm sorry, Mr.—"

"Winterburn. Ronald Winterburn."

"—Mr. Winterburn, but since the president isn't in Los Angeles right now, that phone isn't even here. The phone company brings it and plugs it in when the president comes to town."

"Well, when is he expected?"

"I don't know."

"You're in charge of this hospital and you don't know when to expect the president?"

"No."

The look he gives me makes me add, "I'm sorry."

"I'll just have to find out for myself then, won't I? But I'm getting used to that. If you want something done right, you do it yourself."

And he turns and marches back the way he came, pressing the staff button that opens the doors from our side without a moment's hesitation.

Big Tim follows slowly after.

Calvin Bixby is shaking with silent laughter, and I give him a withering glance.

I am just starting down the corridor again to look in on Dorothy Strickland when the biocom begins to crackle, and I pause to listen. I recognize the voice of the young RA attendant on Unit 5 who brought in Daniel Martin, the flail chest victim: "Man found comatose from carbon monoxide poisoning in underground garage of Metro Building. Blood pressure two-forty over sixty. Victim convulsing and respiration accelerated. ETA, three minutes."

I look up at the clock. The Metro Building, a new forty-story office complex, is, fortunately, less than half a mile away.

This could be a bad one.

The hemoglobin (red blood cells) of the human body have a fatal attraction for carbon monoxide. In fact, our hemoglobin has an affinity about 250 times greater for carbon monoxide than it does for oxygen. So the CO molecules will displace the O_2 molecules, forming carboxyhemoglobin.

I always wonder if people who commit suicide by ingesting CO know about the body's rapacious appetite for this deadly vapor. I suspect they do. Most people who decide to take their own lives carefully research the possible ways to do it.

One patient who tried to kill herself with CO I especially remember from the days I was working in an ER in Las Vegas: Jane Patterson. She was a seventy-seven-year-old woman who reinforced for me the understanding I was beginning to develop then of the cycle of life.

Mrs. Patterson was tired. Her husband had died a decade earlier; her children had little time for or interest in her, or she in them. She had come to Vegas's gaming tables to "win it all, or lose it all."

She lost.

So, at three o'clock in the morning, she went to the RV (Recreational Vehicle) parking lot outside Harrah's, lit a small fire of charcoal briquets on a hibachi inside her van, and lay down and went to sleep.

There is no street or parking lot in Vegas that somebody doesn't walk on every two or three minutes. A passerby smelled the fumes, broke into her van, and brought her to the emergency room.

"Lord, I guess I'm still glad to be here," Jane said when we brought her around. "But the dreams I was dreaming—well, I was young again. They say, you know, CO is the sweet way to go."

But as the poisonous CO permeated her system, I think her dreams might have turned into nightmares. The effects of CO follow a debilitating spectrum cascading downward: first headache; then impaired judgment; dizziness, nausea, and vomiting; collapse; coma and convulsions; respiratory failure, depressed heartbeat, and death. And the shape you survive in depends on how far down the spectrum you go.

That man the RAs are bringing in now is convulsing, so it makes the prognosis grim. He must have been absolutely sure about wanting to die before he chose the underground garage of the Metro Building on a Saturday night as the place to do it. It's amazing he was discovered at all.

He'll need inhalations of 100 percent oxygen; manni-tol if there is cerebral edema; corticosteroids; phlebotomy followed by blood transfusions if he's as severe as I think he is.

I tell Calvin Bixby to get the inhalation therapist down here again stat, and then to call the lab and tell them to stand by for immediate cross-matching.

Illana is already preparing the bed in the trauma room. Watching from the doorway, I feel a sudden rush of gratitude for her skill and the technology instantly avail-able to me, the equipment at my fingertips in that room.

And when the RA unit pulls up to the ambulance entrance, I'm standing at the opening doors, then running beside the gurney as the two attendants wheel it toward the trauma room.

But I am not prepared to look down and see that the man on the gurney is Michael Malone.

Time blurs. I am immobilized, and I don't know how long I stand there, don't know how to measure moments like this.

I remember being in a similar void when I watched my father die, thinking a thousand thoughts and thinking nothing. Yet it wasn't like this because then I couldn't do anything—and now, now I'm expected to do everything. But what do I do with my feelings? They are immobilizing me. I don't know what to do.

I hear someone, I think it is Alfred, say my name, and then suddenly I am functioning again; I am—Dr. Sword, and I am running beside the gurney into the trauma room.

2:44 A.M.—Michael's skin is dusky; his lips are blue; his breathing is quick, shallow, noisy. Even as we wheel him into the trauma room, he convulses on the gurney, hard, jerking muscular spasms. When the convulsion is over, I put my hand on his jaw and try to turn his head, feeling the muscular rigidity I already know is there.

The seconds it takes to position the gurney next to the Stryker bed stretch and stretch. The RA attendants don't meet my eyes, don't say anything. As we lift him in unison onto the bed, he seems so light. How could Michael be this light?

All at once I am aware my entire staff is there—Illana, Alfred, Eugene, Ramon, and, standing back away from the bed, Calvin. I start giving the orders, my voice scarcely above a whisper. "He's going to need intubation and pressurized breathing, one hundred percent oxygen. Let's get some bloods for the usual, plus a carboxyhemoglobin level, plus have him typed and crossed for six units.

"Alfred, start the second IV. Illana, give him Decadron, ten milligrams IV, and start a mannitol drip of a hundred grams. And he needs a Foley catheter and an NG [nasogastric] tube.

"Calvin, call Jill Malone. Tell her to come in."

"What should I tell her?"

"Nothing. Just tell her to get down here as soon as possible and maybe bring a friend."

"Do you want to talk to her?"

"I can't right now."

I examine Michael's pupils with a flashlight beam. They are dilated and barely responding.

I check his pain threshold by sticking a pin deep in his index fingers and the soles of his feet. No response. I rub my knuckles as hard as I can against his breastbone until my skin almost rubs off my knuckle. Again, no response.

"He's deep, too deep," I whisper.

"Pulse one-ten, BP ninety over seventy. Respirations eight and shallow." Illana's voice.

We need to intubate him so we can control his breathing. Usually I can intubate a patient in ten to fifteen seconds, as I did with the flail chest victim. But Michael's neck and jaw are locked into such a rigid spasm I can barely open his mouth.

I ask Alfred to help me move him up a little on the bed so I can get behind him; then I insert the six-inch-long curved blade that opens the jaw and slides over the tongue at the same time. I look for the epiglottis, the vocal cords, trying to hyperextend his neck to bring his mouth more in line with the trachea, but it's no use, his jaw is too rigid. I can't do an endotracheal.

"Nasotracheal," I murmur, and the tube is placed in my hand. Quickly I measure the tip of Michael's ear to the tip of his nose, mark that distance on the tube, then put the tube through his nose down to the mark I have made on the tube. I wait for Michael to draw in a breath, then I shove the tube down his windpipe and listen.

If I hear Michael breathe, I am okay, I'm in the trachea. If I don't hear him breathe, then I'm in the esophagus, and his breathing will stop. In that case I'll have to pull the tube out and try again. The second elongates into empty space.

I pull the tube back out, wait for Michael to take another breath, try again; pause, listen, breathe out deeply myself as I hear Michael exhale. I'm in.

The inhalation therapist is at my elbow. "Get him on the Bird," I say. "Force-breathe him to get rid of some carbon dioxide. Then get a set of blood gases."

I look around for Calvin. "Have we got type-specific blood from the lab?" I demand.

"It's too soon," he replies. "They're—"

"The hell it's too soon!"

I am not being reasonable and I know it, so I stop a moment to pull myself together. A phlebotomy—drawing out his blood and transfusing him with fresh blood—is the only thing left that might help,

I look back down at Michael. He is hooked up to the Bird machine now. There is an IV in his left arm, another in his right; a catheter is in his penis; tubes run out of both nostrils.

But I know the equipment that I was so grateful for minutes ago is not enough.

I glance at the clock. "Start the phlebotomy," I say. And then to Calvin, "Go up there and get the blood."

Even as he turns to leave, there is the sound of running footsteps in the corridor. The lab technician from upstairs hurries in carrying units of blood for the transfusion.

Eugene begins the phlebotomy; Alfred readies the blood for the transfusion.

And then the moment that I have been dreading arrives. The machines are performing their functions and Michael is being monitored by my staff. There is nothing more I can do.

2:55 A.M.—The RA attendants who brought Michael in are in the corridor, drinking coffee, telling Calvin in subdued voices what happened. One of them is just a kid. I can tell he is brand new on the job.

"Jesus," he is saying, "that has to be one of the weirdest things I've ever done, driving the ambulance down into that place. It was empty, you know, on every level. His car was parked on the bottom, way off in a corner. And you know the way the driving lane circles down, like a spiral. We had the flasher on to warn anybody who might be driving up out of the garage—only there wasn't anybody else, just us going down, with that red light flashing on the walls."

"Who found him?" Calvin asks.

"One of those flukey things," the older attendant replies. "Some guy half stoned, thought he was in the garage of the Bonaventure Hotel across the street. He gets down to the bottom level, sees the car, hears the motor running, figures the driver is leaving, and decides to ask for a ride back up to A level. Said he never got unstoned so fast in his life."

"It was so goddam eerie down there," the first one says. "The place is lit, you know, but it's this sick, yellowish light. And there are all those pillars, and it's, well, it's underground, you know?"

I don't want to listen any more.

3:07 A.M. Eugene is back out at the triage desk.

Calvin Bixby is answering the phone, monitoring the teleautograph.

Alfred is moving back and forth among the three patients in the main treatment room, Harold, Roy, and Richard Mudge.

Illana is in the trauma room where Michael remains at the lowest extreme of the coma scale. The Bird is doing most of his breathing.

Ramon has gone to the all-night burger stand near the hospital as he does every night at this time to pick up hamburgers, french fries, milkshakes.

I walk up and down the corridor, wandering through the treatment rooms, hoping for a patient, any kind of patient.

I get one at 3:20.

It's a kid who can't be more than sixteen. He isn't even sick, and there's nothing written on his chart except "Talk to him." That Eugene let him through tells me how hard Eugene is waiting for word about Michael.

"It's my girl friend," the boy tells me.

"She's the one who's sick?" I ask. Sometimes we get requests for house calls, especially at night.

"She isn't sick. She needs—well, some birth control pills."

I just stare at him.

He is embarrassed, but his eyes plead with me. "Please."

"I don't give prescriptions for nonemergency situations," I explain gently. "She would need a physical examination by a family doctor."

"It is an emergency, doc, believe me, it is."

I shake my head. "Look. There are all-night drugstores. You can buy condoms, foam."

"She won't use no foam, and I ... I ..."

But already his urgency is ebbing. I've had requests like this before. It's hard to hold on to eroticism in an emergency room. And probably his girl friend is soundly sleeping wherever he left her.

He gives a sigh and stands up to leave. I almost wish he'd stay, argue with me. I need someone to talk to. An offensive drunk would be nice; someone I could vent my frustration on.

I walk with the boy out to the corridor, and the tele-autograph begins to chatter with Harold's lab results. As I suspected, he's going to have to go in for a liver scan, and I go into the main treatment room to tell him.

His antennae have been working well . . . he knows about Michael. "Listen, I'm laying here, doc," he says, "and I'm praying just as hard as I know how. I'm sending messages to that man in there, 'You can make it, brother, I know you can make it.'"

Christ, I can't seem to handle compassion right now. I draw the curtain around Harold's bed and just stand there with my eyes shut. Harold doesn't speak, and after a minute I'm all right.

"Listen, Harold," I say, "you've got to go upstairs again."

"Yeah, that's what I figured. I wish it was the end of the month, though, instead of the beginning. I usually give a little party when I get my disability check."

When I open the curtains, I see Richard Mudge has set up a small chessboard on his bed, the kind travelers take; the squares on the board have holes, and the chess pieces are mounted on little sticks that fit into the holes. Mudge is studying the board intently, writing figures in a small spiral notebook.

He notices me watching. "I'm designing a chip for chess players," he explains. "But the computer will only make moves based on logic, so to keep player interest up, I have to program some moves that are illogical. That nurse gave me a good one." He nods his head toward Alfred at the other end of the room, with Roy.

"You play chess?"

I nod. I played chess quite a bit in Ethiopia. But the older I get, the less interested I seem to be in games.

"Maybe you'd like to make the next move?" he offers.

I look down at the board, and, studying the pieces, see

there is a knight in danger, so I move it out of harm's way.

Mudge clucks his tongue and takes the knight with the bishop in a move I didn't see at all. "That, too, was an illogical move." He frowns. "But I can't use it."

I go to the other end of the room to see how Roy is doing. He's still staring at the ceiling, but he turns his head when I am next to his bed, his eyes engaging mine briefly.

Alfred says softly, "I think he's coming back."

I nod, hoping so.

When I enter the corridor, Calvin tells me, "Jill Malone's in the waiting room."

4:05 A.M.—The waiting room is almost empty now. A middle-aged woman, poorly dressed but clean, sits passively in front of the television screen. The picture is in vertical roll, probably has been for hours. I can see the telltale layers of clothing the woman is wearing. She isn't carrying a bag; instead she has a newspaper-wrapped bundle tied with yarn. Big Tim isn't supposed to allow vagrants in here, but sometimes despair gets to him just as it does to the rest of us.

Jill is sitting one seat away from Dorothy Strickland, staring into space. Dorothy is watching her with a concerned expression, and I sense she has spoken to her, trying to help.

Jill sees me and stands up. She's wearing the Irish knit sweater I saw on the coat rack in the apartment; her eyes are unnaturally wide, bright with fear. I wonder if she's slept at all since Friday.

"How is Michael?"

I am aware that Dorothy Strickland is listening.

I tell Jill the truth. "Not good."

She turns her head away. Lord, she is so young. She could be my daughter.

"I've been thinking about—about the first time I saw him on the beach," she says. "He was sitting near me talking to someone, waving a popsicle around, forgetting to eat it—and plop, the end of it dropped right in my lap. I screamed and he said, 'Oh, don't you like raspberry?' "

That's the Michael I knew once, too. I almost smile.

"He used to make me laugh all the time." She looks right at my eyes. "But I wasn't really fooled, you know, because under all that I guess he was the saddest man I ever met. Maybe it's even why I married him. I don't know. I was just a kid and I—thought I could help."

She starts to cry softly, and I put my arms around her.

"Can I see him?" she asks.

I hesitate, trying to figure out what's best for her. My eyes meet Dorothy Strickland's. "Sure," I say. "Come on back."

I pause long enough to tell Dorothy that Roy seems to be coming around.

She nods with a little smile at both of us. "He usually does by morning."

4:20 A.M.—Ramon arrives with our food and spreads it out on the cot in the doctors' room, as is the custom.

I tell Illana to go and eat if she wants to, that I'll stay in the trauma room with Michael and Jill, but she says no. She came down so hard on Malone when he was beginning to burn out. Does that make it worse for her now? I think not. It's as bad as it can be for everybody, because Michael is one of us.

I go into the doctors' room.

There is usually something vitalizing about the smell of hamburgers and french fries at four o'clock in the morning, and this is often a noisy, sociable time for my staff— parceling out the foil-wrapped burgers, arguing about who ordered onions and who didn't. It's a ritual that separates us from our patients—we can eat this awful junk food, and they can't—and perhaps for that reason it affirms the sense of family we have working the night shift.

But we're quiet this morning as we gather around the food. So the hospital sounds seem louder than usual: the rustle of the plastic waste bags as the night custodian removes them from the receptacles; the barely discernible aquarium sound the Bird machine makes in the trauma room; the clang of the custodian's bucket against a table leg; the teleautograph chattering (Calvin Bixby leaves to monitor it).

He returns to tell me Richard Mudge's lab tests are all "normal plus," meaning he is, as I already knew, in superb physical condition. I'll offer him a sleeping pill when I send him home, but I doubt he'll accept it. "It is illogical to take medicine when you can't sleep," I can hear him say. Well, perhaps he's right.

"Dr. Sword . . ."

Illana is standing in the doorway.

"Michael has stopped breathing. The machine is doing it all now. His pupils are fixed and dilated."

I get up, walking with her into the trauma room.

Jill's face is white. She's staring at the man on the Stryker bed. But he isn't Michael any more. It's only a body whose functions are being performed by several machines.

I say softly, "Jill, I think we should let him go." She's barely old enough to give consent.

"How can I?" Her voice has a strange, reedy sound to it.

"Because," I say softly, "Michael isn't here any more."

Her head goes down and her hands come up to her face. When she can speak, she says, "Out in the waiting room, I kept trying to call him back, but I knew I wasn't getting through. He couldn't hear me. I guess the truth is I—we lost him weeks ago." Then she whispers, "Yes. Let him go."

I signal the inhalation therapist to take Michael off the machine.

Jill walks quickly out of the room. Illana follows, and, putting an arm around the younger woman's shoulders, walks down the corridor with her.

After a few minutes, Ramon comes in, beginning to remove the catheters, the IV lines, and nasotracheal tubes, and I hear him murmur something, soft Spanish syllables I don't understand the meaning of, though I intuit they are words of farewell.

When everything has been disconnected, I stay for a moment, watching Ramon sheet Michael's body.

I don't have any tears for Michael. I cried all my tears for him—was Friday only yesterday? It seems much longer.

But I feel such a sense of loneliness.

Michael was here, and now he is not.

He was my co-physician; he was once my friend. And he was also, as I began to realize when I talked to Allen on Friday, my threatened self, myself in the shadows.

4:32 A.M.—I go to give Richard Mudge the results of his lab tests and to tell him he might as well go home. But he's asleep.

Alfred comes to stand beside his bed, telling me with

a small smile, "I just sat down and started playing chess with him. You know, all he needed was some company."

Mudge is snoring softly. Asleep, he looks much younger.

4:43 A.M.—Roy Strickland is getting dressed to leave. He knows who he is and where he is, and asks for his wife. Alfred goes to get her.

When Dorothy comes back into the main treatment room, she and Roy embrace briefly, and he murmurs something to her I can't hear, but she nods and gives a little smile.

Then Dorothy turns to me and asks, "What happened to that young girl's husband, the one who—"

"He died."

She sighs and turns back to Roy. "Honey, you buttoned your shirt wrong."

Roy looks down, beginning to undo the buttons.

I go back out into the corridor.

5:55 A.M.—Calvin Bixby tells me I have a long-distance call from Cincinnati.

I frown. Cincinnati? I tell him I'll take it in the doctors' room.

"This is Dr. Sword."

"Good morning, Dr. Sword. This is Dr. Tomkins at the ER at St. Francis." His voice sounds as tired as I feel.

"Yes?"

"A Mr. William Cowan asked me to call you to tell you he had his appendix removed at seven-thirty this morning."

I smile.

"He also asked me to ask you to tell a nurse named Illana that his daughter is beautiful."

I smile some more. "Listen," I say, "that's great."

I summon Illana into the doctors' room and deliver the message from Mr. Cowan.

She smiles too, and then she starts to cry; in a moment she's brushing the tears away, trying not to cry any more.

I put my arms around her and we just hold each other for a few minutes.

"I don't know what's going on in here, but we could use a little help."

Calvin Bixby is standing in the doorway.

Illana and I go out into the corridor.

There are two new charts in the rack.

"Nothing urgent," Calvin murmurs. "I'm just a frustrated top sergeant at heart."

I start to reach for the first chart in the rack, hesitate, turn, and walk down the corridor to the ambulance entrance.

I think the sun is probably just about to come up, and I'd like to watch it.

* * *

*   *   *

Randall and Sandra Sword are now in the process
of putting their marriage back together again.